ISBN

9798305010671

Copyright © 2025, by Brandon Nelson. All Rights Reserved.

Published by Allegro Business Solutions, LLC

OTHER TITLES IN THE "SMALL BUSINESS SUCCESS" SERIES

Small Business, Big Data: Harnessing AI for Smarter Operations and Bigger Profits

C Corporation Unlocked: A Small Business Entrepreneur's Guide to Growth and Taxes

The Small Business Money Manual

Bookkeeping, Taxes, and Financial Strategies Made Simple

TABLE OF CONTENTS

Introduction   1

Part One: Bookkeeping

Chapter 1: What is the Best Way to Keep Track of My Business Finances?   5

Chapter 2: Do I Need to Hire a Bookkeeper, or Can I Manage It Myself?   18

Chapter 3: What is the Difference Between Cash Basis and Accrual Accounting?   28

Chapter 4: What is a Chart of Accounts, and How Do I Set One Up for My Business?   44

Chapter 5: How Do I Track and Categorize Business Expenses Effectively?   60

Chapter 6: How Often Should I Reconcile My Bank Accounts?   76

Chapter 7: How Do I Generate and Interpret Financial Reports?   84

Chapter 8: How Can I Ensure My Books Are Accurate and Up to Date?   100

Chapter 9: What Records Should I Keep, and For How Long?   116

Part Two: Taxes

Chapter 10: What are the Benefits of Setting Up My Business as a Sole Proprietorship, Partnership, LLC, S-Corp, or C-Corp?   131

Chapter 11: Should I Pay Myself a Salary or Take Owner's Draws? 149

Chapter 12: What Expenses Are Tax-Deductible for My Small Business? 164

Chapter 13: How Do I Claim the QBID (Qualified Business Income Deduction)? 192

Chapter 14: How Can I Estimate My Quarterly Tax Payments Accurately? 206

Chapter 15: What Are the Key Tax Deadlines I Need to Know? 220

Chapter 16: How Do I Collect and Remit Sales Tax for My Business? 230

Chapter 17: How Does the IRS View Cryptocurrency Transactions for Tax Purposes? 246

Chapter 18: What Records Do I Need to Keep for Tax Audits? 262

Chapter 19: What Tax-Saving Strategies Can I Use to Reduce My Liability Legally? 277

Conclusion 295

Appendices

Appendix 1: Sample Chart of Accounts 298

Appendix 2: Tax Deadlines and Calendars 304

Appendix 3: Resources for Small Business Owners 308

INTRODUCTION

Welcome to *The Small Business Money Manual: Bookkeeping, Taxes, and Financial Strategies Made Simple.* If you're reading this, you're probably a small business owner or someone who wants to start a business. That's exciting! But figuring out how to handle your money? That can feel a little overwhelming. Don't worry—this book will help you make sense of it all.

Running a small business is a big job. You have to make products, serve customers, and grow your brand—all while keeping track of your finances. Managing money isn't just about staying out of trouble with taxes. It's the secret to making your business successful and stress-free. When you take control of your bookkeeping and taxes, your business can grow and thrive.

I've worked with many small businesses over the years. I've seen how bad financial habits, like missing tax deadlines or losing track of expenses, can hurt a business. But I've also seen how understanding the basics of bookkeeping and taxes can make a huge difference. My goal is to make these topics simple and practical so you can apply them to your business right away. Learning these skills will help you avoid mistakes, grab opportunities, and build a solid foundation for your future.

What's in This Book?

This book is divided into two parts to make it easy to follow:

- **Part I: Bookkeeping**: This section covers the basics of tracking your money. You'll learn how to set up a bookkeeping system, create a Chart of Accounts, and organize your expenses. We'll also look at how to create financial reports that tell you if your business is doing well or needs improvement. Whether you do this yourself or hire someone to help, this section will give you the tools to stay organized and save time.

- **Part II: Taxes**: Taxes don't have to be scary. In this section, we'll go over what taxes your business needs to pay and how to keep more of your money by using deductions and smart strategies. We'll also talk about things like choosing the best type of business structure and dealing with cryptocurrency. Planning ahead will help you avoid surprises and make tax time much easier.

A Guide to Solve Your Problems

Each chapter in this book answers a common question small business owners face. Whether you're trying to balance your books, figure out how much tax to pay, or prepare for an audit, you'll find clear and simple answers here. This isn't just about following rules. It's about giving you the confidence to make decisions and take charge of your business.

When you understand your finances, you'll be able to plan for the future, make smart choices, and feel more secure. Managing money isn't just about numbers. It's about building the business you've always dreamed of and setting yourself up for success.

Let's Get Started

Now it's time to begin! Whether you're new to business or have been at it for years, this book is here to help you take control of your finances. With the right tools and strategies, you'll not only meet your challenges—you'll go beyond what you thought was possible.

Your journey to financial success starts here. Let's get to work and make your business everything you want it to be!

PART I: BOOKKEEPING

Chapter 1: What is the Best Way to Keep Track of My Business Finances?

Section 1: Understanding the Importance of Financial Tracking

Keeping track of your business money is one of the most important jobs you have as a business owner. It's not just about writing down numbers; it's about understanding what those numbers mean and using them to make smart decisions. Whether you're working alone, have a small team, or just getting started, keeping good financial records helps you:

- **Watch Your Cash Flow**: Knowing how much money is coming in and going out helps you pay your bills, invest in your business, and avoid running out of money. Good cash flow management lets you plan ahead and act quickly if needed.

- **Know If You're Making Money**: Keeping track of your finances shows if your business is earning a profit and which products or services are doing the best. This helps you focus on what works and grow your business smarter.

- **Be Ready for Taxes**: Accurate financial records make filing taxes easier and help you avoid penalties for mistakes. Staying on top of taxes means less stress and fewer surprises when it's time to file.

- **Get Loans or Investments**: If you need money to grow, lenders and investors will ask to see your financial records. Having organized records shows you're professional and know how to manage money.
- **Plan for the Future**: Good financial data helps you spot trends, cut unnecessary costs, and plan for growth. It also helps you decide things like hiring employees, expanding, or buying new equipment.

Why Small Businesses Struggle with Financial Tracking

Many small business owners find financial tracking hard or think it takes too much time. Some don't know where to start, while others believe they only need to track finances for taxes. Unfortunately, ignoring this responsibility can cause big problems, like running out of money, missing tax deadlines, or even failing altogether.

Not keeping track of your finances is one of the top reasons small businesses fail. Without knowing your financial situation, you might think you're doing better than you are or miss important deadlines. Starting with simple systems and good habits can make tracking easier and save you time in the long run.

Steps to Good Financial Tracking

Here are some tips to keep your finances organized:

1. **Keep Business and Personal Money Separate**: Don't mix personal and business expenses. Open a business bank account and get a business credit card. This makes it easier to track spending and prepare accurate reports.

2. **Set a Regular Schedule**: Make tracking your finances a habit. Whether you do it daily, weekly, or monthly, staying consistent helps you catch issues early and avoid last-minute stress.

3. **Use Good Tools**: Choose bookkeeping software that works for your business. Tools like QuickBooks, Xero, or Wave can automate tasks, reduce mistakes, and save time.

4. **Learn Basic Accounting Terms**: Even if you hire someone to help, knowing terms like income, expenses, assets, and liabilities can help you understand your finances better. This knowledge makes conversations with bookkeepers or accountants more helpful.

5. **Keep All Receipts and Records**: Save your receipts, invoices, and other financial documents. These are important for tax time and in case of an audit. Use digital tools to scan and organize your paperwork.

6. **Review Reports Often**: Look at reports like profit and loss statements and balance sheets to see how your business is doing. Regular reviews help you spot problems, measure progress, and adjust your plans.

7. **Ask for Help When Needed**: If managing finances feels overwhelming, hire a bookkeeper or accountant. Professionals can offer advice and make sure you're following the rules. Their help can save you time and prevent costly mistakes.

The Big Picture

Tracking your business finances may not be the most exciting part of owning a business, but it's one of the most important. By staying organized and making financial management a priority, you'll make better decisions and feel more confident about your business. Accurate records also build trust with banks, investors, and tax authorities.

Good financial tracking helps you adapt to changes. Whether it's a drop in sales, an unexpected bill, or a new chance to grow, having the right data helps you handle it. In the next sections, we'll share tips and tools to make tracking easy and effective. By the end of this chapter, you'll know how to set up a system that keeps your business on track and helps you reach your goals.

Section 2: The Basics of Keeping Track of Your Money

Knowing how to keep track of your business finances is super important for growing your business and keeping it strong for the future. If you don't track your finances properly, you could face fines or miss chances to make smart decisions for your business. This section will cover the basics: keeping personal and business finances separate, picking the right tools, and building good habits.

Keeping Personal and Business Finances Separate

The first step in managing your business finances is making sure your personal and business money don't mix. Mixing them up can cause messy records, lost tax deductions, and problems if your business gets audited. Here's how to avoid that:

1. **Get a Business Bank Account:** A business account is not just a smart idea—it's often required if you have an LLC or corporation. This account makes it easy to track all money coming in and going out of your business, which makes bookkeeping simpler.

Having a business account also helps you look more professional to clients, vendors, and banks. It can help you get loans, better deals with suppliers, and more trust from customers.

2. **Use a Business Credit Card:** A business credit card keeps your business expenses separate and can come with perks like cashback or travel rewards. These cards also often have tools for tracking spending and creating reports, which can help during tax time.

Keeping your business credit separate can also protect your personal credit score if your business runs into money troubles. It's also helpful if you want to give cards to trusted employees to manage their spending.

3. **Don't Mix Payments:** Don't use business funds to pay for personal expenses, or vice versa. If you make a mistake, fix it right away by recording the error and transferring money between accounts. This keeps your records clean and helps you follow tax laws.

Picking the Right Tools to Track Finances

The tools you choose for managing your business money can save you time and effort. Here are some popular options:

1. **Accounting Software:** Programs like QuickBooks, Xero, and Wave help you track income, expenses, invoices, and payroll. They often connect to your bank accounts and provide reports for tax season. Many of them have mobile apps, so you can update your records anytime.

These tools also come with advanced features like automated bank reconciliation and reports you can customize. They're a great investment as your business grows.

2. **Spreadsheets:** If your business is just starting, a well-organized Excel or Google Sheets file can work. But as your business grows, this option may become too time-consuming and prone to mistakes. Spreadsheets need constant manual updates and don't have the smart features of accounting software.

For business owners who are comfortable with formulas, spreadsheets can still be a flexible and affordable choice, especially for short-term projects.

3. **Expense Tracking Apps:** Apps like Expensify or Mint let you track receipts and organize expenses easily. These are great for entrepreneurs who travel a lot or make frequent purchases. Many apps can also connect to your accounting software for a smooth tracking system.

Some apps have extra features like mileage tracking, receipt scanning, and automatic sorting of expenses. These save time and reduce errors.

4. **Bookkeeping Services:** If managing your finances feels overwhelming, hiring a bookkeeper can help. Many bookkeepers use software you can access, so you get professional help and still have control over your accounts.

Hiring a bookkeeper lets you focus on growing your business while knowing your finances are in good hands.

Building Good Habits

No matter what tools you use, success depends on consistency. Even the best systems won't work if you don't keep them updated. Here are some tips to help you stay on track:

1. **Set Up Regular Check-Ins:** Spend time each week or month reviewing your financial records.

Use this time to check bank statements, organize expenses, and see how much money is coming in and going out. Regular check-ins help you catch problems early and make better decisions.

Set reminders to make this a habit. Staying on top of your records also makes tax season less stressful.

2. **Save All Receipts:** Keep receipts in a safe place, either digitally or physically. This is important for accurate records and audits. Many apps let you scan and store receipts, which saves space and makes them easier to find.

Try to organize receipts by categories like travel, meals, or supplies. Some digital tools can even pull the important info from receipts automatically.

3. **Automate Tasks:** Use automatic bank feeds, recurring invoices, and scheduled payments to save time and avoid late fees. Automation reduces the chances of mistakes and helps you stay organized.

Look for more ways to automate, like setting up alerts for unusual transactions or integrating payroll systems. These tools make managing your money easier.

4. **Track Key Numbers:** Keep an eye on important financial numbers like your profit margin, money owed to you, and bills you need to pay. Understanding these numbers helps you make smart changes. For example, knowing your profit margin can help you adjust prices or cut costs.

Checking these numbers regularly also helps you plan for future expenses and investments. You might even create a dashboard to see all these metrics in one place.

By building strong habits and using the right tools, you can keep your business finances on track. This not only helps with taxes but also prepares your business to grow and compete. In the next section, we'll talk about good ways you can keep track of your finances.

Section 3: What Bookkeeping Software is Best for Small Businesses?

Choosing the right bookkeeping software for your small business can make a big difference in how well you manage your money. With so many options out there, the best choice depends on what your business needs, what kind of work you do, and how much you know about accounting. Here, we'll explain what to look for and highlight some popular choices.

Things to Think About When Picking Software

1. **Easy to Use:** If you don't have much experience with accounting, look for software that is simple and easy to understand. Pick a program with clear instructions and tools that guide you through tasks. Some even include step-by-step tutorials to help you get started.

2. **Features and Room to Grow:** Think about what your business needs now and what it might need in the future. Basic features like tracking

expenses and creating invoices are important, but you might also want tools for managing inventory, handling payroll, or letting other team members use the software. Choose something that can grow with your business.

3. **Cost:** Prices for bookkeeping software can vary. Some programs charge as little as $10 a month, while others have higher costs for advanced features. There are free options, but they may not include everything you need as your business grows. Always consider if the software is worth the price in the long run.

4. **Cloud or Desktop:** Cloud-based software lets you access your account from anywhere and automatically updates itself. This can be helpful if you work in different places. Desktop software is usually a one-time purchase and may be more secure if you prefer keeping your data offline, but it's less flexible.

5. **Works with Other Tools:** If you already use other tools like online stores, payment systems, or customer management programs, make sure the bookkeeping software works well with them. This will save time and help avoid mistakes by keeping all your data connected.

6. **Support and Training:** Good customer support can be a lifesaver when you're getting started or run into problems. Look for software that offers support by phone, chat, or email, and has helpful

guides or videos. Some even offer live training sessions to teach you how to use the program.

Popular Bookkeeping Software Choices

1. **QuickBooks Online:** QuickBooks Online is one of the most popular tools for small businesses. It has many features, like tracking expenses, sending invoices, and creating financial reports. It can grow with your business and connects with lots of other apps. Plans start at $30 a month.

2. **Xero:** Xero is another great option that's easy to use and has strong reporting tools. It supports unlimited users and includes features like bank account matching, tracking projects, and payroll tools. Plans start at $13 a month, making it affordable for many small businesses.

3. **Wave:** Wave is a free option that works well for small businesses or startups. It includes basic features like tracking income and expenses, creating invoices, and scanning receipts. However, it doesn't have advanced features like inventory management or time tracking. Paid services like payroll are available if you need them.

4. **FreshBooks:** FreshBooks is designed for service-based businesses like consultants or freelancers. It's great for tracking time, managing clients, and creating professional-looking invoices. Plans start at $17 a month. While it's

very easy to use, it's not the best choice if you need advanced tools for payroll or inventory.

5. **Zoho Books:** Zoho Books is part of a larger set of tools from Zoho. It's a good choice if you already use other Zoho products. It offers features like managing inventory, setting up automatic workflows, and handling taxes. Plans start at $15 a month, making it a budget-friendly option.

6. **Sage Business Cloud Accounting:** Sage is a simple solution for small businesses just starting out. It helps with basic tasks like connecting your bank accounts and creating simple reports. Plans start at $10 a month, so it's a good choice if you're switching from spreadsheets and want an affordable option.

7. **Kashoo:** Kashoo is straightforward software that's easy to use for small businesses with simple needs. It's ideal for freelancers or businesses that don't need a lot of extra features. Plans start at $20 a month, and users praise its helpful customer support.

Steps to Choose the Best Option

1. **Figure Out What You Need:** Make a list of features you use now and ones you might need later. Think about your industry's specific needs, like tracking inventory for a store or managing projects for a contractor.

2. **Try Free Trials:** Many software providers let you try their tools for free. Use this time to see how easy it is to use and if it fits the way you work.

3. **Read Reviews:** Look at what other people say about the software, especially those in your line of work. They can share tips and point out things you might not notice.

4. **Ask for Advice:** Talk to other business owners, accountants, or bookkeepers. Their experiences can help you pick the best option.

5. **Think About the Future:** Choose software that can grow with your business so you don't have to switch later. Look for features like multi-user access and affordable plans that work as you expand.

Conclusion

Choosing the right bookkeeping software can save time, lower stress, and make sure your financial records are accurate. QuickBooks Online is a top choice for many small businesses, but options like Wave, Xero, and FreshBooks might fit your needs better. Take the time to review your choices, test features, and find the software that will help your business succeed. The effort you put in now will lead to smoother financial management down the road.

Chapter 2: Do I Need to Hire a Bookkeeper, or Can I Manage It Myself?

Section 1: Assessing Your Bookkeeping Needs

As a small business owner, deciding whether to manage your bookkeeping yourself or hire a professional is a big decision that can affect your business's finances. Both options have their pros and cons, and the right choice depends on how big your business is, how complicated its finances are, and how comfortable you are with managing money. This section will guide you through figuring out what your bookkeeping needs are so you can make the best choice. Taking time to think about this now can help you avoid mistakes and stress later.

Step 1: Look at How Complex Your Business Is

Start by thinking about how your business operates. Ask yourself these questions:

- How many sales or purchases do you make each month? If you handle a lot of transactions, you might need better tools and more help to stay organized.

- Do you sell products, services, or both? Keeping track of inventory and pricing can make bookkeeping harder, especially if you're selling in multiple ways.

- Do you work in more than one state or country? Different tax rules and currency conversions can add extra challenges.

If your business is more complex, it might be worth hiring a professional to help. Having someone with experience can make sure your records are accurate and follow all rules.

Step 2: Think About Your Skills and Time

Your own skills and the time you have available are important when deciding if you should handle bookkeeping yourself. Ask yourself:

- **How much do I know about bookkeeping?** Are you comfortable using bookkeeping software and understanding basic financial terms? If not, you might make mistakes or miss ways to save money.

- **Do I have enough time?** Bookkeeping needs regular attention, often taking hours each week or even every day. If you're already busy running your business, it might be better to hire someone so you can focus on other things. Ignoring your books because you're too busy can lead to costly mistakes later.

Being honest about your skills and time will help you make the right choice for your business. It's okay to admit if you need help—it's better than being overwhelmed.

Step 3: Look at Your Budget

Your budget can play a big role in whether you hire a bookkeeper or do it yourself. The cost of professional help depends on how complicated your business is and what kind of help you need. Here's what to consider:

- **Software Costs:** If you do it yourself, you'll probably need bookkeeping software like QuickBooks, Xero, or Wave. These tools can make the job easier, but they still take time to learn and use.

- **Professional Fees:** Bookkeepers can charge by the hour, by the month, or for specific tasks. Prices can range from a few hundred dollars a month for simple services to more for full financial management.

- **Potential Savings:** Hiring a professional might cost more upfront, but it could save you money in the long run by preventing mistakes and finding ways to save on taxes. Errors can lead to fines or missed tax deductions, which can cost more than hiring help.

Understanding these trade-offs will help you choose the most cost-effective option for your business.

Step 4: Get the Right Tools and Resources

Whether you handle bookkeeping yourself or hire someone, you'll need the right tools to manage your finances. Here's what you should think about:

- **Accounting Software:** Programs like QuickBooks, Xero, and Wave can help you track your money, create reports, and balance your accounts. Look into the features of each to find one that works best for your needs.

- **Learning Resources:** If you're doing it yourself, take advantage of guides, tutorials, or online courses to build your skills. Many free or low-cost resources can teach you the basics.

- **Professional Support:** Even if you don't hire a bookkeeper full-time, it's helpful to have an accountant or financial advisor you can call for advice. Building these relationships can help you solve problems as they come up.

- **Backup Systems:** Make sure your records are stored securely, either in the cloud or on a physical device. Losing your data can be a disaster, so having backups is very important.

Using the right tools and resources will help you keep your books in good shape, whether you're doing it on your own or getting help from a professional.

Step 5: Make the Best Choice for Your Business

After thinking about how complex your business is, your skills, your time, your budget, and the tools you have, you're ready to decide. Some people start by doing their own bookkeeping and hire a professional later when the business grows. Others hire help from the beginning to make sure everything is done right from day one.

Remember, your decision doesn't have to be final. You can change your approach as your business evolves. For example, you might handle the books yourself during the startup phase but hire a bookkeeper once your revenue grows or your finances get more complicated.

No matter what you choose, staying consistent is key. Whether you're doing the work yourself or working with a bookkeeper, keeping accurate and up-to-date records is essential. Good bookkeeping is the foundation of a successful business and helps you make smarter decisions. It gives you a clear picture of your finances, keeps you compliant with tax laws, and helps you take advantage of opportunities. Taking these steps now will set your business up for long-term success.

Section 2: How to Assess a Bookkeeper's Qualifications

Finding the right bookkeeper is an important part of keeping your business's finances on track. A good bookkeeper can help you keep accurate records, follow tax laws, and save time. But how can you tell if someone is the right person for the job? Let's break it down into simple steps to make the process easier.

1. Relevant Experience

The experience a bookkeeper has can show how well they'll handle your business's needs. If they've worked with businesses like yours, they'll probably understand your challenges better. For example, a bookkeeper for a retail store might be great with tracking sales tax and inventory, while one for a service business could know more about billing clients and managing payroll.

What to Ask:

- Have you worked with businesses like mine before? If yes, how long?
- How many years have you been doing bookkeeping?
- Do you have experience with tasks my business needs, like handling taxes in multiple states or managing subscription payments?

Also, find out if they can adjust to more complicated finances as your business grows.

2. Certifications and Training

Some bookkeepers have certifications that show their skills and dedication. Not all bookkeepers get certified, but those who do may know more about the latest tools and rules. Certifications like QuickBooks ProAdvisor or Certified Bookkeeper (CB) can be useful.

What to Ask:

- Do you have any bookkeeping certifications?
- Are you trained in using popular software like QuickBooks, Xero, or Sage?
- How do you keep up with changes in tax rules and financial tools?

Ask if they've taken extra courses or training to stay current. This shows they're serious about their work.

3. Technical Skills

A good bookkeeper should know how to use technology to make their job easier. Tools like accounting software, spreadsheets, and even data dashboards can save time and reduce mistakes.

What to Ask:

- What accounting software are you most comfortable using? Are you familiar with cloud-based tools?
- Have you set up any automated processes, like creating invoices or reconciling bank accounts?
- Can you create and explain reports that show how my business is doing financially?

Check if they can connect bookkeeping tools with other systems you use, like payroll or inventory software.

4. Attention to Detail and Accuracy

Being detail-oriented is one of the most important skills for a bookkeeper. Even small mistakes can lead to bigger problems with your finances or taxes. A great bookkeeper knows how to spot errors and fix them quickly.

What to Ask:

- How do you make sure your work is accurate?
- Can you tell me about a time you caught and fixed a mistake before it became a bigger issue?

- How do you handle tasks like reconciling accounts to make sure everything matches?

You might even ask for a sample of their work or have them do a quick test to see how well they manage detailed tasks.

5. Communication and Availability

A bookkeeper isn't just someone who works with numbers. They're also part of your team. That means they need to explain financial information in a way you can understand and be available when you need them.

What to Ask:

- How do you usually share updates and reports with clients?
- When are you available if I have questions or need something quickly?
- How do you explain complicated financial topics to someone who doesn't know much about accounting?

Ask for references to learn more about their communication style and how reliable they are.

6. References and Reviews

Talking to past clients can help you understand if the bookkeeper is dependable and does good work. Online reviews can also give you a better idea of their reputation.

What to Ask:

- Can you give me contact info for past clients who can talk about your work?
- Have you received any reviews or testimonials?
- Can you share an example of a tough problem you solved for a client?

When you follow up with references, ask about how well they meet deadlines, solve problems, and work with others.

7. Cost and Value Alignment

While finding the right skills is important, you also need to make sure the bookkeeper's rates fit your budget. Some charge by the hour, while others charge a flat monthly fee. Make sure you understand what's included so there are no surprises.

What to Ask:

- What are your rates? Do you charge hourly, monthly, or per project?
- Are there extra fees for things like tax preparation or software costs?
- How do you show clients the value of the work you do?

Having this conversation upfront will help you avoid misunderstandings later on.

By looking at these factors, you'll be able to pick a bookkeeper who's the right fit for your business. They'll not only handle your current needs but also support you as your business grows.

Chapter 3: What is the Difference Between Cash Basis and Accrual Accounting?

Section 1: Definitions and Examples

To understand the difference between cash basis and accrual accounting, it helps to start with simple definitions and examples. These two methods are used to track money in a business, but they work in different ways. Let's break them down and explore them in detail so you can see how each approach might impact your financial decisions.

Cash Basis Accounting

Cash basis accounting is the easier of the two methods. In this system, you record money only when it's actually received or spent. This means:

- Income is recorded when you get paid, not when you send an invoice.
- Expenses are recorded when you pay a bill, not when you receive it.

This method works a lot like keeping track of your personal budget, which is why many small businesses like it. It provides a straightforward way to manage finances without dealing with complex calculations or timing issues.

Example: Imagine you own a landscaping business. In October, you finish a $5,000 job for a client, but they don't pay you until December. With cash basis accounting, you would record the $5,000 as income in December because that's when you got the money.

Similarly, if you buy a lawnmower for $2,000 in November but don't pay for it until January, the expense would be recorded in January when the payment is made. This method focuses on tracking money as it comes in and goes out.

Why Small Businesses Like It: Many small businesses prefer cash basis accounting because it's simple and shows exactly how much cash is available at any given time. It's a great way to keep a close eye on your immediate financial situation without worrying about what's owed to you or what you owe to others. However, it doesn't always give a full picture of your overall financial health.

Accrual Accounting

Accrual accounting takes a different approach. In this system, you record income and expenses when they happen, even if no money has changed hands yet. This method gives a clearer picture of how your business is doing because it matches income and expenses to the time they are earned or incurred.

Example: Using the same landscaping business, let's say you complete the $5,000 job in October and send the client an invoice. With accrual accounting, you record the $5,000 as income in October, even though you don't get paid until December. If you buy a lawnmower for $2,000 in November and get an invoice, you would record the $2,000 expense in November, even if you pay in January. This method matches income and expenses to the months they actually happen, giving a better understanding of profitability over time.

Why It's Helpful: Accrual accounting is especially useful for businesses that need to track long-term performance or manage complex transactions. It provides a better sense of how your business is really doing by showing both money you're owed and money you owe, even if cash hasn't moved yet. This can help with planning, budgeting, and making strategic decisions.

Key Differences Highlighted

1. **Timing of Transactions**: The biggest difference is timing. Cash basis tracks money only when it moves, while accrual accounting tracks income and expenses as they happen. This means cash basis might not show all your obligations or expected revenue, while accrual accounting does.

2. **Simplicity**: Cash basis accounting is easier to use and great for businesses with simple finances. Accrual accounting is more complicated but gives a fuller view of your business. With accrual accounting, you need to manage additional records and keep track of receivables and payables.

3. **Financial Accuracy**: Accrual accounting shows a more accurate picture of your business's financial health. It includes money you're owed and bills you need to pay, which helps you plan

better. Cash basis, on the other hand, might show that you have plenty of money, even if you have big unpaid bills.

4. **Rules and Requirements**: Some larger businesses or those with inventory are required to use accrual accounting by law. Smaller businesses often have the option to choose, but it's important to understand the implications of both methods.

Practical Implications

When you understand these two methods, it's easier to see how they affect your finances. Cash basis accounting is great if you want something simple and easy to manage. It's particularly useful for service-based businesses or those with straightforward transactions. Accrual accounting, on the other hand, helps you get a clearer idea of how your business is doing overall. This can be especially helpful for planning and reporting.

Which Businesses Benefit Most? Cash basis is often best for businesses that prioritize simplicity and don't deal with complex transactions. This includes freelancers, consultants, and small businesses without inventory. Accrual accounting is a better fit for businesses with inventory, larger operations, or those looking to understand their long-term financial performance. It's also ideal for companies seeking investors or loans, as it provides a more complete financial picture.

Tax Considerations: Your choice of accounting method can also affect your taxes. Cash basis might let you delay income recognition to lower taxes in a given year, while accrual accounting provides a clearer and often more consistent financial picture for tax purposes. Always consult with a tax professional to make the best choice for your situation.

In the next section, we'll look at the pros and cons of each method to help you decide which one is the best fit for your business.

Section 2: Advantages and Disadvantages of Cash Basis and Accrual Accounting

Choosing between cash basis and accrual accounting can feel overwhelming, but understanding the pros and cons of each method makes it easier. These accounting systems affect how a business tracks its money, plans for the future, and handles taxes. Let's dive deeper into both methods, exploring their benefits and challenges in greater detail so you can confidently determine which one suits your business best.

Cash Basis Accounting

Advantages:

1. **Easy to Use:**
    - Cash basis accounting is simple to understand and set up, making it perfect for small businesses or individuals who don't have much accounting experience.

- Transactions are recorded only when money is actually received or paid, keeping things straightforward and easy to follow without requiring extensive bookkeeping knowledge.

2. **Clear View of Cash Flow:**
    - It shows exactly how much cash you have on hand at any time, helping you manage your day-to-day operations effectively without needing complicated financial analysis.
    - This method is especially helpful for businesses with tight budgets or unpredictable income streams, giving owners confidence in managing available resources.

3. **Flexible for Taxes:**
    - You only report income when it's received, so you might be able to shift some income to the next tax year if needed, which can help with tax planning and reduce liabilities.
    - This can be a big help for businesses with seasonal income or uneven cash flow, allowing owners to manage tax burdens more effectively.

4. **Low Cost to Maintain:**
   - Since cash basis accounting is straightforward, it's usually cheaper to manage. You may not need expensive software or professional help, making it ideal for startups or sole proprietors with limited resources.
   - It's quick and easy to keep up with, leaving you more time to focus on growing your business or addressing other priorities.

Disadvantages:

1. **Not the Full Picture:**
   - This method doesn't track money that you're owed (accounts receivable) or bills you haven't paid yet (accounts payable), which can lead to gaps in understanding your true financial health.
   - Without these details, it's harder to see long-term trends or make accurate projections for growth and investments.

2. **Tax Surprises:**
   - If you get a lot of payments at the end of the year, your taxable income might suddenly jump, possibly pushing you into a higher tax bracket.

- This could lead to unexpected tax bills, putting a strain on your cash reserves if you haven't planned ahead.

3. **Not Great for Big Businesses:**
    - Larger businesses or those with inventory often need more detailed financial records, which cash basis accounting doesn't provide. Inventory management, in particular, requires tracking costs over time.
    - Regulations might even prevent bigger companies from using this method, especially as they grow or seek external funding.

4. **Not Accepted Everywhere:**
    - Cash basis accounting doesn't follow Generally Accepted Accounting Principles (GAAP). If you're looking for investors or loans, this might be a problem since lenders often require GAAP-compliant reports that show a fuller financial picture.

Accrual Accounting

Advantages:

1. **Detailed Financial Picture:**
    - Accrual accounting records money when it's earned and expenses when they happen, even if no cash has changed

hands yet. This offers a complete and accurate view of your financial health.

- By capturing all transactions, accrual accounting helps you see the bigger picture of your business performance over time.

2. **Better for Planning:**

    - With detailed records, you can make smarter decisions about budgets, investments, and growth strategies. Knowing exactly what's owed to you and what you owe others makes long-term planning more reliable.
    - This method is particularly useful for businesses with complex operations, such as those managing multiple contracts or long-term projects.

3. **GAAP Compliant:**

    - Accrual accounting follows GAAP rules, which is important if you're seeking investors, loans, or other external funding. GAAP compliance makes your financial statements credible and professional.
    - Investors and lenders are more likely to trust your financial data, increasing your chances of securing support.

4. **Matches Income and Expenses:**
   - This method connects income to the expenses it took to earn it, giving a clearer idea of profitability and operational efficiency.
   - It's especially useful for businesses that handle large projects over months or years, showing the real costs and income for each period.

Disadvantages:

1. **More Complicated:**
   - Accrual accounting is harder to understand and requires more work to maintain. Many businesses need professional help to get it right, which can add to operational costs.
   - Mistakes can happen if you're not careful, and correcting errors might require even more time and expense.

2. **Doesn't Track Cash Directly:**
   - Since it doesn't focus on cash flow, you might look profitable on paper but struggle to pay bills if customers are late with payments or if cash reserves are low.
   - You'll need to monitor cash flow separately to avoid potential liquidity problems.

3. **Higher Costs:**
    - Because it's more detailed, accrual accounting often requires better software or professional accountants, which can cost more. This might be challenging for small businesses with tight budgets.
    - The extra time and effort required to maintain accuracy also increase operational demands.

4. **Tax Timing Issues:**
    - You may have to pay taxes on income you haven't received yet, which can strain your cash reserves if you're not prepared. This requires careful planning to avoid unexpected cash shortfalls.
    - Keeping track of both taxes and cash flow becomes an additional responsibility for business owners.

By comparing these pros and cons, you can decide which accounting method fits your business needs best. Think about the size and complexity of your business, the resources you have available, and your goals for the future. Picking the right method will help you stay organized, make better decisions, and set your business up for long-term success.

Section 3: Which Method is Right for Your Business?

Choosing between cash basis and accrual accounting depends on your business's size, goals, and needs. To help you make the best decision, let's take a closer look at some key factors and how each method fits different business situations:

1. Size and Complexity of Your Business

- **Cash Basis**: This method works best for small businesses, freelancers, or solo entrepreneurs who want to keep things simple. If your business doesn't deal with inventory or handle a lot of unpaid bills or invoices, cash basis accounting is easy to use and understand. It's especially good for businesses just starting out because it doesn't require much accounting knowledge. You can track your income and expenses easily, making it an excellent choice for service-based businesses or hobby businesses.

- **Accrual Basis**: This method is better for businesses that are growing or have more complicated operations, like managing inventory or offering credit to customers. Accrual accounting tracks money when it's earned or owed, giving you a clearer picture of your business's financial health. For example, if your business regularly sends invoices and offers payment terms, accrual accounting helps ensure you're accurately reflecting revenue and expenses. This method is also ideal for businesses planning to expand or hire employees, as it provides a detailed financial overview.

2. Regulatory and Tax Rules

- **Cash Basis**: The IRS lets most small businesses with annual sales under $27 million use cash basis accounting. This is a good option for service-based businesses without inventory. For example, a freelance graphic designer or a dog-walking business could use cash basis without any issues. But if your business involves buying and selling products or holding inventory, you might be required to use accrual accounting to follow IRS rules. This is because inventory accounting requires matching income with expenses, something cash basis doesn't easily handle.

- **Accrual Basis**: Larger businesses or those needing detailed financial reports for banks or investors usually have to use accrual accounting. If you plan to file audited financial statements or meet specific tax rules, this method ensures you're following the regulations. For instance, if your business operates internationally or has complex supply chains, accrual accounting might be necessary to meet legal requirements. Consulting a tax professional is a smart move to make sure you're compliant with current regulations and avoid potential penalties.

3. Understanding Financial Reports

- **Cash Basis**: This method makes it easy to see how much cash you have because it only tracks money when it comes in or goes out. But it doesn't show the full picture of your business's financial obligations, like unpaid bills or expected income. For example, if a customer is late paying you, it won't show up as income until you get the money. This simplicity works well for small businesses that don't need to analyze their finances deeply.

- **Accrual Basis**: This method gives you a more complete picture of your business's finances because it records transactions when they happen. It's helpful for making long-term plans and understanding how your business is really performing. For example, even if cash flow varies due to seasonal sales, accrual accounting shows a clearer picture of profits and losses. This accuracy can help you spot trends, budget better, and prepare for future growth.

4. Managing Cash Flow

- **Cash Basis**: This method makes it easy to track how much cash is available at any time, helping you avoid overspending. For instance, if your business operates on tight cash margins, cash basis accounting can help you make quick decisions about spending. However, it doesn't account for upcoming bills or money you're waiting to receive, which could make planning harder. For businesses that rely on consistent cash flow, this limitation can sometimes cause surprises.

- **Accrual Basis**: This method requires more effort to keep an eye on cash flow since it records income and expenses even if no cash has moved yet. For example, your books might show profits, but your bank account could be low if clients haven't paid yet. To manage this, many businesses using accrual accounting also use tools like cash flow forecasts to plan for future needs. Combining accrual accounting with careful cash management can help businesses balance their short-term and long-term financial goals.

5. Your Business Goals

- **Cash Basis**: If your business is small and you don't plan to grow much, cash basis accounting might be all you need. It's simple to use and takes less time to manage. For example, a local handyman or an artist selling pieces occasionally might find cash basis perfect for their needs.

- **Accrual Basis**: If you want to grow quickly, attract investors, or take on loans, accrual accounting gives you detailed and accurate financial information. This method is often required by banks, investors, and stakeholders because it meets standard accounting rules (GAAP). For example, if you're a small manufacturer planning to launch a new product line, accrual accounting ensures you're fully aware of your business's financial commitments. It's also better for businesses planning mergers or big funding opportunities since it shows the true financial health of the business. Accrual accounting helps you build trust with stakeholders by presenting a clear and accurate financial picture.

Final Thoughts

Cash basis accounting is easier to use, but accrual accounting is better as businesses grow or need more detailed financial reports. Deciding which method to use depends on your business's current situation and future plans. Talking to a bookkeeper or accountant can help you make the right choice.

Many accounting software programs let you create reports using both methods, so you can compare and analyze your finances. This flexibility can help you manage cash flow while also getting the detailed insights of accrual-based reports. Choosing the right accounting method will give you the confidence to make smart decisions and lead your business to success. No matter what you choose, understanding how each method works can help you take control of your finances and set your business up for a brighter future.

Chapter 4: What is a Chart of Accounts, and How Do I Set One Up for My Business?

Section 1: Explanation of a Chart of Accounts (COA)

A Chart of Accounts (COA) is a basic yet essential tool in bookkeeping and financial management. It organizes and lists all the financial activities of a business in a structured way. Think of it as a detailed map for your accounting system that helps you keep track of your money by grouping it into key categories such as income, expenses, assets, liabilities, and equity. This organization makes it much easier to understand where your money is coming from, how it's being used, and where it's going.

The COA acts like a master list of all the accounts your business uses to manage its finances. Each account is given a special number or code, which simplifies the process of recording transactions and looking up financial details. These codes often follow a logical system that groups related accounts together, enabling you to easily find and analyze specific information about your finances. For example, all your expense accounts might start with the number "5," while all your income accounts might start with "4."

A good COA ensures your financial transactions are recorded in a clear, consistent way. This consistency is crucial when creating financial reports like profit and loss statements, balance sheets, or cash flow statements. These reports are essential for understanding how your business is performing and planning for the future. A well-organized COA also ensures you follow tax laws and other regulations, helping you file your taxes accurately and avoid errors that could result in penalties or fines.

Why is a COA Important?

1. **Clear Organization:** A COA organizes your financial data in a logical and systematic way, making it easier to find and understand. With a clear system, you can quickly locate specific transactions, check account balances, or review financial data without confusion.

2. **Accurate Reports:** By categorizing your financial records properly, you can create accurate reports that comply with accounting and tax rules. These reports give you a clear picture of your business's financial health and help you make well-informed decisions.

3. **Better Decision-Making:** A well-structured COA allows you to analyze your business performance in specific areas, such as tracking how much you're spending on marketing or how profitable a product line is. This helps you identify what's working, where you can cut costs, or where you might want to invest more resources.

4. **Audit Ready:** If your business is audited, a detailed and organized COA makes it easier to provide proof of your transactions. Auditors will

appreciate the clarity and structure, saving you time and stress during the process.

5. **Grows With Your Business:** As your business expands, your COA can be adjusted to include new accounts or categories. A well-designed COA will scale with your business, keeping your financial tracking effective and efficient as your operations grow.

Structure of a COA

A COA is typically divided into five main sections:

1. **Assets:** These are things your business owns that have value, such as cash, accounts receivable (money customers owe you), inventory, and equipment. Assets are usually split into two categories: current assets (which can be converted to cash within a year, like bank accounts or inventory) and non-current assets (long-term items like property, vehicles, or machinery).

2. **Liabilities:** These are debts or obligations your business owes to others, such as loans, unpaid bills (accounts payable), or taxes. Liabilities are also divided into current liabilities (debts due within a year) and long-term liabilities (debts that will be paid off over a longer period).

3. **Equity:** This represents the owner's share of the business and includes money you've invested and any profits you've kept in the business (retained earnings). Equity shows how much of

your business's assets you truly own after all debts are paid.

4. **Income:** This is the money your business earns from selling products or providing services. Examples include categories like "Sales Revenue," "Service Revenue," or "Other Income."

5. **Expenses:** These are the costs of running your business, such as rent, employee wages, utilities, and supplies. Expenses can be further divided into fixed costs (which stay the same regardless of activity, like rent) and variable costs (which change based on business activity, like raw materials).

Each of these sections can be broken down into smaller subcategories to provide even more detail. For example, under "Expenses," you might have subcategories like "Advertising," "Office Supplies," "Travel," or "Utilities." This level of detail helps you track exactly where your money is being spent and identify areas where you might save or need to invest more.

You can also customize your COA to suit the specific needs of your business. For example, a retail store might have accounts for "Cost of Goods Sold" and "Inventory Shrinkage," while a consulting firm might focus on accounts like "Professional Fees" and "Client Retainers." Tailoring your COA ensures that it reflects the unique financial activities of your business.

In summary, a Chart of Accounts is an essential tool for organizing and managing your business's finances.

Whether you own a small startup or a growing company, a well-planned COA helps you stay on top of your financial records, make informed decisions, and prepare for growth. By customizing your COA to fit your business's needs, you can ensure your records are accurate, compliant with regulations, and useful for planning your next steps. A well-maintained COA is not just about staying organized—it's about setting your business up for long-term success.

Section 2: Steps to Create a COA Tailored to Your Business

Making a Chart of Accounts (COA) for your business is an important step in keeping your financial records organized. A clear and well-structured COA helps you track all the money flowing into and out of your business, understand how your business is performing, and prepare for tax filing. By following these detailed steps, you can create a COA that fits your business's unique needs and is flexible enough to grow with you.

1. Understand Your Business Operations

Before creating your COA, take time to think about how your business operates. Ask yourself questions such as:

- What products or services does your business offer?

- What are your main sources of income? Is it product sales, service fees, or something else?

- What types of expenses do you have regularly? For instance, do you spend on materials, advertising, rent, or utilities?

- Are there any special financial rules or reporting requirements you must follow, such as industry regulations or expectations from investors?

Having a thorough understanding of your business operations ensures that your COA will include all the accounts you need while avoiding unnecessary ones. This helps you stay organized and focus only on the financial areas that matter.

2. Choose an Accounting Method

Your accounting method determines how you record financial transactions, and this will affect your COA. Decide which method suits your business:

- **Cash Basis Accounting**: This method records income when you receive payment and expenses when you pay bills. It's straightforward and ideal for smaller businesses.

- **Accrual Accounting**: This method records income when it is earned and expenses when they are incurred, even if no money has changed hands yet. It provides a more complete picture of your finances and is often used by larger businesses.

Choosing the right method ensures your COA includes the correct accounts, such as accounts receivable and accounts payable if you're using accrual accounting.

3. Set Up Main Account Categories

A standard COA is divided into five main account categories. These categories form the backbone of your financial system:

1. **Assets**: These are things your business owns that have value, such as cash, inventory, equipment, or property.
2. **Liabilities**: These are obligations your business owes, such as loans, credit card balances, or unpaid bills.
3. **Equity**: This represents the owner's investment in the business and any profits that are retained.
4. **Revenue**: This is the money your business earns from selling products or providing services.
5. **Expenses**: These are the costs of running your business, such as rent, utilities, payroll, and supplies.

Make sure these categories reflect your business activities so that your financial reports are accurate and helpful.

4. Add Subcategories for Details

To make your COA more useful, add subcategories under each main account. This provides more detailed tracking. For example:

- **Assets**: Include subcategories like Cash, Accounts Receivable, Inventory, Vehicles, and Equipment.

- **Liabilities**: Add subcategories such as Credit Card Debt, Business Loans, and Payroll Liabilities.

- **Revenue**: Break it down into Product Sales, Service Income, and Interest Income.

- **Expenses**: Use detailed subcategories like Rent, Utilities, Payroll, Marketing, Travel Costs, and Technology Expenses.

The level of detail depends on your business needs. The more specific your subcategories are, the easier it will be to see where your money comes from and where it goes.

5. Use Account Numbers

Assign numbers to your accounts to keep everything organized. A numbering system makes it easier to find and update accounts. A common format is:

- **1000-1999**: Assets
- **2000-2999**: Liabilities
- **3000-3999**: Equity
- **4000-4999**: Revenue
- **5000-5999**: Expenses

For instance, you might assign 1010 to Cash, 1020 to Accounts Receivable, and so on. Leave space between numbers so you can add new accounts later as your business grows.

6. Test Your COA

Before you start using your COA, test it with sample transactions. This helps you find and fix any problems. Check that:

- All income and expense categories are included.
- Transactions can be recorded and tracked easily.
- Financial reports like Profit and Loss Statements and Balance Sheets are accurate and provide useful insights.

Testing your COA ensures it works smoothly before you rely on it for real financial tracking.

7. Keep Your COA Updated

Once your COA is set up, document it in a way that is easy to understand. Write brief descriptions for each account to explain what belongs there. For example, you might note that "Office Supplies" includes items like pens, paper, and printer ink.

Review your COA regularly to keep it current. As your business grows or changes, you may need to add new accounts or adjust existing ones. For example, if you introduce a new product line, you might need to create new revenue and expense accounts to track it.

8. Use Accounting Software

Modern accounting software can simplify creating and managing a COA. Programs like QuickBooks, Xero, and Wave often come with pre-made COA templates that you can customize. Using software helps you:

- Save time by automating repetitive tasks.
- Reduce errors with built-in checks and balances.
- Generate financial reports quickly and accurately.

As your business becomes more complex, software makes it easier to keep your finances organized and up-to-date.

By following these steps, you can create a Chart of Accounts that meets your business needs. A well-designed COA is a powerful tool that helps you manage your finances, make informed decisions, and plan for the future. Taking the time to set it up properly now will pay off as your business grows and succeeds.

Section 3: Common COA Categories for Small Businesses

A well-organized Chart of Accounts (COA) is like the foundation of your financial system. It divides all your financial transactions into clear groups, making it easier to see how your business is doing. By using a COA, you can keep track of your money, follow accounting rules, and make smarter financial decisions. Below are the common COA categories that most small businesses use, along with examples of what goes in each category. Understanding these categories will help you manage your business finances better.

1. Assets

Assets are things your business owns. These accounts show your resources and investments. Assets are usually divided into current assets, which can turn into cash quickly, and fixed assets, which are long-term items you use in your business.

- **Current Assets**
    - Cash and Cash Equivalents: Money in your checking accounts, petty cash, and short-term investments
    - Accounts Receivable: Money that customers owe you for goods or services
    - Inventory: Products or materials you have ready to sell or use
    - Prepaid Expenses: Payments for things like rent or insurance that you made in advance
- **Fixed Assets**
    - Equipment: Machinery, computers, furniture, and tools your business uses
    - Vehicles: Cars, trucks, or other vehicles your business owns
    - Real Estate: Buildings, warehouses, or land your business owns

- Accumulated Depreciation: A record of how much value your fixed assets have lost over time due to use or wear

Keeping track of your assets helps you know the value of what your business owns and plan for future investments or upgrades.

2. Liabilities

Liabilities are what your business owes to others, like banks, vendors, or lenders. These accounts help you stay on top of your financial responsibilities and are divided into current liabilities (short-term) and long-term liabilities.

- **Current Liabilities**
  - Accounts Payable: Money you owe suppliers for goods or services
  - Short-Term Loans: Loans or credit lines that you need to pay back within a year
  - Accrued Expenses: Costs like wages, utilities, or taxes that you owe but haven't paid yet

- **Long-Term Liabilities**
  - Loans Payable: Mortgages or other loans that take more than a year to pay off

- Lease Obligations: Long-term agreements for renting equipment or property

Managing your liabilities helps you keep cash flow healthy and avoid missed payments.

3. Equity

Equity shows the owner's share of the business. It is what's left after subtracting liabilities from assets. Equity accounts track contributions, profits, and withdrawals by the owner(s).

- Common Accounts:
  - Owner's Equity: The money or assets the owner(s) invested in the business
  - Retained Earnings: Profits that the business keeps instead of paying out to the owner(s)
  - Distributions/Draws: Money the owner(s) take out of the business for personal use

Equity accounts help business owners see their financial stake and decide on reinvesting or expanding.

4. Revenue

Revenue accounts track the money your business earns. These accounts make it easier to see how much income you're bringing in and identify trends over time.

- Common Accounts:
    - Sales Revenue: Money earned from selling products or goods
    - Service Revenue: Income from providing services, like repairs or consulting
    - Other Income: Extra money earned from interest, rent, or selling assets

Revenue accounts show how well your business is performing and help you plan for future growth.

5. Expenses

Expense accounts track the money your business spends to run and grow. They are divided into operating expenses and non-operating expenses.

- **Operating Expenses**
    - Cost of Goods Sold (COGS): Direct costs of making or buying the products or services you sell
    - Salaries and Wages: Payments to employees, including benefits and payroll taxes
    - Rent or Lease: Costs for using office, retail, or storage spaces
    - Utilities: Bills for electricity, water, internet, and other services

- Marketing and Advertising: Spending on ads, promotions, and campaigns
- Office Supplies: Items like paper, pens, or software that you use every day

- **Non-Operating Expenses**
  - Interest Expense: Costs of borrowing money, like loan interest
  - Depreciation and Amortization: The gradual loss of value of your tangible or intangible assets over time

Tracking your expenses helps you find areas where you can save money and decide where to invest more.

6. Other Accounts

Some businesses may need extra accounts for specific needs, like taxes or owner transactions.

- **Taxes**
  - Sales Tax Payable: Money you collect from customers and owe to the government
  - Income Tax Payable: Taxes your business owes on its profits
- **Owner Contributions and Distributions**
  - Loans to/from Owners: Tracking money lent to or borrowed from the owner(s)

Other accounts can include donations, grants, or special funds depending on your business type.

Tips for Customizing Your COA

1. Use these basic categories as a starting point, and adapt them to fit your business needs.
2. Keep it simple by combining similar items to avoid creating too many detailed accounts.
3. Work with a bookkeeper or accountant to make sure your COA meets tax and industry standards.
4. Review your COA regularly to keep it relevant as your business grows or changes.

By using these categories and adjusting them to your needs, you can create a COA that helps you manage your finances, make smarter decisions, and plan for a successful future.

Chapter 5: How Do I Track and Categorize Business Expenses Effectively?

Section 1: Why Categorizing Expenses Matters

Organizing your business expenses into clear categories is a key part of good money management. It helps keep your financial records neat, makes it easier to understand your business's money situation, and supports smart decision-making. Categorizing expenses also helps you follow tax rules, prepare budgets, and plan for the future. Let's explore why this is so important in detail:

1. Better Understanding of Spending

Sorting expenses into categories like office supplies, utilities, travel, and marketing helps you see exactly where your money goes. This makes it easier to spot patterns and control costs. For example, if your electricity bills keep going up, you might look into ways to save energy and lower those costs. Clear records also stop you from overspending and help keep your cash flow steady, so your business can stay on track. Additionally, understanding spending habits can reveal hidden inefficiencies. For instance, grouping office supply expenses might show that buying in bulk could save money in the long term.

2. Accurate Financial Reports

When you categorize expenses correctly, your financial reports, like profit and loss statements, are easier to understand and use. These reports show how well your business is doing and can guide decisions about spending and saving. Lenders, investors, and other important people also rely on these reports to see if your business is strong enough to support loans or investments. Good categorization also helps you track important numbers, like how much you're spending compared to how much you're earning, so you can make changes if needed. Categorized reports also provide insights that help you evaluate trends over time, such as whether rising costs are cutting into your profits or if certain investments are yielding positive returns.

3. Easier Tax Filing

Properly categorizing expenses makes it clear which costs can be written off on your taxes. This can lower the amount of income you have to pay taxes on. For example, business meals, travel, and home office expenses might be deductible. Clear categories reduce mistakes and make it less likely you'll face an audit. Organized records also save time when you're filing taxes and help you handle tricky situations, like managing taxes in different states. Additionally, understanding tax-deductible categories ensures you don't miss out on opportunities to save money. For instance, knowing that professional development expenses can often be deducted might encourage you to invest in training programs that benefit your business.

4. Smarter Budgeting and Planning

When you compare your spending to your budget, you can see where things don't match up. For example, if you keep spending more on advertising than you planned, you can look into why and adjust for the future. Categorized expenses also make it easier to predict future costs. If you know how much you've spent in the past, you can plan budgets that make sense. This helps you spend money on the things that matter most for your business. Over time, detailed budgeting supported by well-organized expense categories can help you make more ambitious plans for growth, such as opening a new location or expanding your product line.

5. Supports Business Growth

As your business grows, your finances can get harder to handle. Categorizing expenses keeps things organized so you can keep up. This system helps you see what's driving your costs, set goals, and make choices based on real data. For example, knowing how much money goes into research and development can help you focus on new ideas. Having clear expense records also makes it easier to attract investors, who often want to see detailed financial information before giving you money. Additionally, strong financial records can help you qualify for grants or government programs aimed at supporting small businesses.

6. Following Rules and Building Trust

Many industries have specific rules about how businesses should report their finances. Categorizing expenses properly helps you follow these rules and avoid fines. It also shows that you're running your business professionally, which builds trust with customers, partners, and regulators. For example, if you're in an industry that requires certain costs to be reported separately, organized records make sure you're meeting those standards. Beyond compliance, professionalism in financial management signals stability and reliability, helping you secure better partnerships and deals with suppliers or collaborators.

7. Boosting Decision-Making Confidence

When you have a clear view of your expenses, you can make smarter decisions with more confidence. Knowing exactly how much you're spending in different areas helps you decide where to cut back or where to invest more. For instance, if your analysis shows that spending more on digital ads has a direct link to higher sales, you can confidently increase your advertising budget. Similarly, spotting areas of overspending, like excess travel costs, can lead to policies that save money without sacrificing quality.

Real-Life Example

Imagine a small business owner who doesn't categorize expenses. At tax time, they can't figure out which costs qualify for deductions, so they miss chances to save money. Their financial reports are also messy, making it hard to see where improvements are needed. This can lead to overspending or not investing enough in important areas like marketing. On the other hand, a business with organized expense categories can file taxes easily, learn from clear financial reports, and make smart decisions. For example, they might see that online ads bring in good profits, so they decide to spend more in that area and cut back on less useful costs.

Additionally, clear records can help them quickly apply for a small business loan to fund an expansion, increasing their chances of success.

In Summary

Categorizing business expenses isn't just about staying organized—it's a smart way to run your business. It helps you manage money better, save on taxes, and make strong plans for the future. By keeping detailed and categorized records, you not only simplify daily financial tasks but also lay the groundwork for achieving long-term business goals. Whether you're running a small shop or a growing company, putting effort into categorizing expenses will pay off by keeping your business financially healthy, more efficient, and ready to grow.

Section 2: Best Practices for Tracking

Tracking your business expenses the right way is important to keep your business running smoothly and follow tax rules. Keeping good records helps you stay organized, manage your money, and have accurate information for bookkeeping and taxes. Here are some simple and effective tips to help you track expenses better and avoid common pitfalls that can lead to financial problems.

1. Use a Separate Business Account

The first thing you should do is keep your personal and business money separate. Open a business checking account and only use it for business purchases. This makes it easier to keep track of all your expenses in one place. Having a separate account also makes your business look more professional and can help if you ever need to apply for a loan or credit. When your business transactions are isolated, it's easier to spot patterns and understand where your money is going. It also simplifies tax preparation since personal expenses won't accidentally get mixed in.

2. Record Expenses Right Away

Don't wait to write down your expenses. Keep track of them as soon as you spend money. Doing this will help you avoid mistakes, keep from losing receipts, and stay on top of your records. Recording your expenses right away also helps you see how much money you've spent, so you can make decisions quickly if you need to cut costs. If you're not ready to log everything immediately, use a notebook, mobile app, or even voice notes to jot down details until you can enter them in your system.

3. Keep Digital Copies of Receipts

Paper receipts can get lost or damaged, so it's a good idea to take pictures or scan them. Use apps or cloud storage to save these digital copies. Many expense apps let you upload and sort receipts, making the process faster and easier. Having digital records also makes things less stressful if you ever need to show proof of your expenses. Some apps even allow you to search by date, amount, or category, saving you time when reviewing past expenses. By digitizing your receipts, you'll create a searchable, organized system that's easy to maintain.

4. Use Expense Tracking Software

Using software to track your expenses can make your life much easier. Tools like QuickBooks, Xero, or Wave can help you keep track of spending, sort expenses into categories, and create helpful reports. These programs often connect to your bank and credit cards, so they automatically update your records. Some even give tips to help you save money or notice spending patterns. Advanced features like real-time reporting and mobile app integration can give you a clear financial picture no matter where you are. Look for software with customization options to tailor reports and tracking to your specific needs.

5. Create Clear Categories

Decide on specific categories for your expenses, like office supplies, travel, or utilities. Stick to these categories to keep things simple and organized. Clear categories also make it easier to find tax-deductible expenses. Review your categories regularly to make sure they match what your business is doing, and add new ones if needed. Having consistent categories helps you see trends over time, such as how much you spend on marketing each quarter. This can help you budget better and make smarter financial decisions.

6. Check Your Bank Statements Often

Make sure your bank records match what you've written down. Check your bank statements every month to spot any mistakes or unexpected charges. This habit helps you catch problems early, like charges you didn't approve, and keeps your records accurate. Regular checks also give you better control over your business finances. If you notice recurring charges that no longer benefit your business, cancel those subscriptions or renegotiate terms. Keeping an eye on your statements also helps you plan for upcoming payments and avoid overdraft fees.

7. Watch Over Petty Cash

If your business uses petty cash for small purchases, set up a system to track it. Keep receipts for every purchase and check the petty cash balance often. You can use a logbook or an app to keep things organized. This helps prevent mistakes and ensures the cash is being used properly. To avoid misuse, limit the amount of petty cash available and set rules about what it can be spent on. Regularly reviewing petty cash transactions helps ensure accountability and prevents financial leaks.

8. Use Business Credit or Debit Cards

Whenever possible, pay with a business credit or debit card. These cards give you detailed statements, which makes tracking expenses easier. Many cards also let you sort expenses by type. Using cards can also simplify reimbursements for employees, and some cards offer rewards, like cashback or travel points, which can save your business money. Be strategic about choosing a card with benefits that align with your business needs, such as rewards for office supplies, fuel, or travel expenses. Using cards also helps build your business credit score, which can be useful if you need financing in the future.

9. Review Your Expenses Regularly

Take time every month or quarter to look at your expenses. Check for spending patterns, mistakes, or places where you can save money. For example, if you see a category where spending is too high, you might renegotiate contracts or switch to cheaper options. Regular reviews help you keep your budget under control and avoid waste. Use these reviews to plan for future expenses, such as scaling your business or preparing for tax payments. Reviewing expenses also helps you stay aware of financial goals and adjust your strategies when necessary.

10. Teach Your Team

If your employees make purchases for the business, give them clear instructions on how to report expenses. Teach them why keeping receipts and using the right categories is important. Training your team regularly helps everyone stay on the same page. You can also give them access to expense apps to make reporting easier. Building a culture of responsibility and transparency makes managing expenses much smoother. Setting clear expectations and providing tools for expense reporting can also reduce errors and prevent delays in reimbursements.

By following these tips, you can keep your business expenses under control and your records in great shape. Good tracking habits make bookkeeping easier, help you plan better, and prepare you for any financial challenges that might come your way. With a solid system in place, you'll be ready to handle growth opportunities and keep your business on track. These practices not only save you time and money but also give you peace of mind, knowing your business finances are in order.

Section 3: Tools and Templates for Efficient Expense Management

Managing business expenses is one of the most important parts of running a successful business. It helps you keep your finances in order, ensures you're ready for tax season, and shows you ways to save money. With the right tools and templates, this task becomes much simpler and more manageable. By using these resources, you can stay organized, follow financial rules, and make smart decisions to grow your business. Below is an expanded guide to the tools and templates that can help streamline expense management.

1. Accounting Software

Accounting software is one of the best ways to track, organize, and report your business expenses. These programs can simplify tasks like preparing for taxes, creating financial reports, and keeping your records accurate. Let's look at some of the most popular options:

- **QuickBooks**: This software is loaded with helpful features. You can link your bank accounts, automatically categorize expenses, and generate detailed reports. It's one of the most widely used tools for small and medium-sized businesses because of its versatility.

- **Xero**: Xero is known for being easy to use and powerful. It offers tools to track expenses, upload receipts, and connect with other business apps. Its cloud-based setup ensures you can access your data from anywhere.

- **Wave**: A completely free option, Wave is perfect for small businesses with tight budgets. Despite being free, it includes robust tools like expense tracking and receipt scanning.

- **FreshBooks**: Tailored for freelancers and small businesses, FreshBooks offers simple tools for tracking expenses and billing clients. Its clean and straightforward design makes it an excellent choice for beginners.

2. Expense Tracking Apps

For those who are always on the go, expense tracking apps are a fantastic solution. These apps allow you to log and categorize expenses anytime, anywhere, ensuring you don't forget anything:

- **Expensify**: This app is excellent for tracking expenses quickly. It lets you scan receipts, automatically sort them into categories, and sync with other accounting tools. It's especially useful for businesses that involve a lot of travel or expense reimbursements.

- **Zoho Expense**: Zoho Expense is a great choice for small teams. You can upload receipts, track mileage, and even get expenses approved by your manager. It also creates detailed reports to simplify audits and reviews.
- **Mint**: While Mint is mainly a personal finance app, it can also be helpful for small businesses. It allows you to set budgets, track spending, and manage your financial goals in an easy-to-use interface.

3. Spreadsheets

If you prefer a more hands-on approach, spreadsheets are an affordable and customizable tool. They're particularly useful for businesses that want to create their own expense tracking systems or have unique needs:

- **Microsoft Excel**: Excel is a powerful tool for manually tracking expenses. You can use its features like formulas, pivot tables, and charts to organize and analyze your data.
- **Google Sheets**: Similar to Excel but cloud-based, Google Sheets allows for real-time collaboration. It's easy to share and edit spreadsheets across teams, making it a great choice for businesses with multiple users.

Sample Spreadsheet Columns:

To create a basic expense tracking spreadsheet, include these columns:

- Date
- Vendor
- Category (e.g., travel, office supplies, utilities)
- Payment Method
- Amount
- Notes

This format captures all the key details you need to keep your expenses organized and easily accessible.

4. Receipt Management Tools

Keeping track of receipts is crucial for managing expenses and preparing for tax audits. These tools can help you digitize and organize your receipts:

- **Shoeboxed**: This tool scans paper receipts and organizes them into digital categories. It also creates expense reports, which are very helpful during tax season.
- **Hubdoc**: Hubdoc automatically collects and stores receipts, bills, and other financial documents. It integrates with your bank and vendors to pull in important files automatically.
- **Dext (formerly Receipt Bank)**: This tool extracts key data from receipts and syncs with accounting software. It's a great choice for businesses that deal with different currencies or frequent transactions.

5. Templates for Expense Management

Ready-made templates are a simple way to start tracking your expenses. They save time and ensure consistency in your records. Here are some useful examples:

- **Monthly Expense Tracker Template**: This template organizes all your monthly expenses by category. It helps you spot spending trends and find opportunities to save money.

- **Travel Expense Report Template**: Designed for tracking travel-related costs, this template includes sections for transportation, lodging, meals, and incidentals. It's ideal for businesses that reimburse employees.

- **Budget vs. Actual Template**: This template compares your planned budget to what you actually spent. It's a great way to stay on track and avoid overspending.

You can download templates from platforms like Microsoft Office, Google Sheets, or financial management websites. Many of these templates are customizable, so you can adapt them to fit your business needs.

6. Integration with Other Systems

To make expense management more efficient, ensure your tools can connect to other systems you use. Integration eliminates duplicate work and keeps your data accurate:

- **Payroll systems**: Link expense tools to your payroll software to track employee reimbursements accurately.

- **Bank accounts**: Connect your expense tracking tools to your bank for automatic imports and sorting of transactions.

- **Tax software**: Sync your expense data with tax software to simplify filing and ensure you're claiming all eligible deductions.

7. Key Features to Look for in Expense Management Tools

When choosing a tool or template, keep these features in mind:

- Automatic categorization of expenses based on your rules.
- Receipt scanning and storage to keep important records safe.
- Customizable reports that provide valuable insights into your spending.
- Integration with other financial tools for a seamless workflow.
- Strong security features to protect your sensitive financial data.

Conclusion

Using the right tools and templates can make managing expenses much simpler and more efficient. Whether you choose advanced accounting software, handy apps, or simple spreadsheets, the key is finding what works best for your business. With these tools, you can save time, avoid mistakes, and keep your finances organized. A good expense management system doesn't just help you stay on top of your finances—it also gives you the confidence to make smarter decisions and grow your business.

Chapter 6: How Often Should I Reconcile My Bank Accounts?

Section 1: Explanation of Bank Reconciliation

Bank reconciliation means checking your business's financial records and comparing them with your bank statements to make sure they match. This important bookkeeping step helps you catch mistakes, fix errors, and keep your records accurate. It's like a checkpoint that ensures your financial data is reliable and helps you make good business decisions. When your records align with your bank statements, you can trust that you're working with a clear picture of your financial health.

When you reconcile your bank accounts, you look for and fix differences between your records and the bank's records. These differences can happen for several reasons, like delays in processing, mistakes, or missing entries. For example, checks you've written might not have cleared yet, deposits could still be in process, or there might be transactions you don't recognize. Small errors, such as recording the wrong amount or forgetting to log a transaction, can lead to bigger problems if they're not caught early. It's also easy to miss things like bank fees, interest, or automatic payments unless you check regularly. Fixing these problems quickly can save you from bigger issues down the road, like overdrafts or inaccurate financial reports.

The main goal of bank reconciliation is to make sure your records show the true financial picture of your business. Accurate records help you manage your cash flow, plan for future expenses, and make informed decisions. When you reconcile often, you can find mistakes like double entries, forgotten transactions, or wrong amounts. It also gives you a chance to spot serious problems like fraud or unauthorized withdrawals, so you can take action right away. Fraudulent transactions, for instance, can go unnoticed for months without regular reconciliation, potentially leading to financial losses that could have been avoided. Regular reconciliation keeps your cash flow accurate, which is critical for planning budgets and managing your money effectively.

Reconciling your accounts has other benefits too. It keeps you accountable by encouraging a routine for reviewing financial information. When you make reconciliation a habit, you're more likely to record your transactions correctly and consistently. This routine helps you stay organized and reduces stress, especially during busy times like tax season. Accurate and up-to-date records mean fewer surprises when preparing taxes and ensure you're in compliance with legal requirements. You'll also save time and effort by not having to go back and fix months of errors all at once.

Many modern bookkeeping programs offer tools to make reconciliation simpler. These tools can match transactions, highlight differences, and create helpful reports. For instance, automated software might identify a missing deposit or flag a transaction that doesn't align with your records. However, even with these tools, it's important to understand what reconciliation is and why it's necessary. Automation can save time, but you still need to review everything to make sure it's right. This is especially important for small business owners who might need to explain their finances to investors, lenders, or accountants. Additionally, understanding the process gives you more control and confidence in managing your business finances.

By reconciling your bank accounts regularly, you protect your financial records and set your business up for success. It helps you build good habits, improve transparency, and feel confident in managing your business's finances. Reconciliation also strengthens your financial awareness, allowing you to identify trends and adjust your strategies as needed. For example, you might notice that certain expenses are higher than expected, prompting you to cut costs or renegotiate contracts. Ultimately, regular reconciliation is more than just a bookkeeping task—it's a way to maintain control over your financial future and ensure your business remains on solid ground.

Section 2: Step-by-Step Guide to Bank Reconciliation

Making sure your bank accounts match your business records is essential for keeping track of your money. It helps you avoid costly mistakes, identify discrepancies, and understand exactly where your finances stand. Here is a detailed guide to walk you through the process of completing a bank reconciliation:

Step 1: Gather What You Need

Before starting, ensure you have all the necessary documents and tools at hand. Being prepared will make the process much smoother and quicker:

- **Your Accounting Records:** These could be maintained in a notebook, spreadsheet, or bookkeeping software like QuickBooks or Xero.
- **Your Latest Bank Statement:** Obtain the most recent statement covering the period you want to reconcile.
- **Supporting Documents:** Gather receipts, invoices, and payment records for the same period to verify transactions.
- **Online Banking Access:** If needed, log into your bank account to cross-check details of recent transactions.

Taking a few minutes to prepare beforehand will save you time and help avoid interruptions during the process.

Step 2: Match the Starting Balances

Begin by confirming that the opening balance on your bank statement matches the opening balance in your accounting records. This step is crucial because any discrepancies at the start can carry forward and complicate the reconciliation process.

- **Check for Old Issues:** Look for prior problems like outstanding checks or recording errors.

- **Use Historical Records:** If balances don't match, review previous reconciliations to pinpoint the source of the error and correct it before moving forward.

Step 3: Review Transactions One by One

Carefully go through each transaction listed on your bank statement and compare it to your accounting records. Match them up line by line:

- **Deposits:** Confirm all incoming funds, such as customer payments, loans, or refunds, are recorded in both places.
- **Withdrawals and Payments:** Verify that every check, transfer, or electronic payment is accounted for in your system.

Mark each matched transaction as you progress. If using software, it might provide tools to simplify this step, such as automated transaction matching. For manual methods, you can use a highlighter or tick marks to keep track.

Step 4: Spot Any Differences

Look for transactions that appear in one record but not in the other. These differences often fall into one of the following categories:

- **Outstanding Checks:** Payments you've recorded but that the bank hasn't processed yet. Keep a list to monitor these later.

- **Deposits in Transit:** Deposits that you've recorded but haven't cleared with the bank yet. Confirm these are accurate and expected to appear soon.

- **Bank Fees and Charges:** These might include account fees, overdraft charges, or wire transfer fees that are not yet in your accounting records. Add them as needed.

- **Errors:** Mistakes can happen in either your records or the bank's statement, such as typos or misentered amounts. Double-check the source.

- **Unfamiliar Transactions:** Investigate any charges or credits that don't make sense. Unfamiliar items might be fraud-related and require immediate attention.

Step 5: Update Your Records

Once you've identified discrepancies, make adjustments to your accounting records to ensure they reflect the actual transactions:

- **Add Missing Items:** Include things like bank fees, interest payments, or forgotten transactions.

- **Correct Errors:** Fix any mistakes, such as incorrect amounts or duplicate entries, to ensure your books are accurate.

- **Track Outstanding Items:** Keep a record of unresolved items like outstanding checks or deposits in transit for future reconciliation.

Document every change thoroughly to maintain a clear record of what adjustments were made and why.

Step 6: Make Sure Balances Match

After making all necessary adjustments, check the ending balances. Your accounting records' closing balance should now match the closing balance on the bank statement.

- **Recheck for Errors:** If they still don't match, revisit the earlier steps to find and fix any overlooked issues.
- **Account for Timing Differences:** Keep in mind that certain items, like outstanding checks, might temporarily prevent the balances from aligning perfectly. Record these items for clarity.

Step 7: Record Your Reconciliation

Once the balances match, prepare a detailed reconciliation report. This report should include:

- **Opening and Closing Balances:** Note the starting and ending balances for both the bank and your accounting records.
- **Outstanding Items:** List any unresolved transactions, such as checks or deposits in transit.
- **Adjustments:** Detail any changes made to fix errors or add missing items.

- **Supporting Documents:** Attach copies of your bank statement and any relevant receipts or invoices.

Proper documentation not only helps with audits but also makes future reconciliations easier.

Step 8: Do It Regularly

Regular reconciliation is key to keeping your records accurate and avoiding major problems down the road. Most businesses reconcile their accounts monthly, but if you have a lot of transactions, consider doing it weekly or even daily.

- **Catch Issues Early:** Regular reconciliations let you find and fix errors quickly, preventing them from compounding.
- **Use Tools and Reminders:** Set up alerts or use features in your bookkeeping software to stay on schedule and simplify the process.

By following this comprehensive guide, you'll keep your financial records accurate, reduce stress, and feel confident about your financial management. Regular reconciliations ensure that your money is where it should be, giving you peace of mind and helping your business thrive.

Chapter 7: How Do I Generate and Interpret Financial Reports?

Section 1: Overview of Key Financial Reports

Financial reports are essential tools for understanding how your business is doing and planning for the future. They show how your company is performing and help you identify trends, risks, and opportunities. By analyzing these reports, you can spot strengths and weaknesses and make smart decisions to guide your business toward success. The three most important financial reports for any business are the Profit and Loss Statement (P&L), the Balance Sheet, and the Statement of Owner's Equity. Learning how to read and use these reports will give you better control over your business's finances and long-term growth.

The Profit and Loss Statement (P&L)

The P&L, also called the Income Statement, shows your business's income, costs, and expenses for a specific period, such as a month, quarter, or year. It provides a clear picture of whether your business is making money and where adjustments may be needed to improve profitability.

Key parts of a P&L:

- **Revenue:** This is the total money your business earns from selling products or services. Revenue can be grouped into categories, like product types or customer segments, to better understand which areas are performing well.

- **Cost of Goods Sold (COGS):** These are the direct costs of making your products or providing your services. Examples include materials, labor for production, and any other expenses directly tied to creating what you sell.

- **Gross Profit:** This is Revenue minus COGS. It shows how much money you're making from your main business activities before subtracting other expenses.

- **Operating Expenses:** These are the costs of running your business that aren't directly tied to production, like rent, utilities, salaries, marketing, and office supplies.

- **Net Profit (or Loss):** This is what's left after subtracting all expenses from Gross Profit. It's your bottom line and shows whether your business is profitable or operating at a loss.

Reviewing your P&L regularly can help you spot patterns, like which months bring in more income or where costs are rising. For example, you might notice that marketing expenses have increased but revenue hasn't improved, signaling the need to evaluate your strategy. This report is key to understanding how well your business turns revenue into profit and finding ways to improve your operations.

The Balance Sheet

The Balance Sheet gives you a snapshot of your business's finances at a specific point in time. It shows what your business owns, what it owes, and the value left for the owner(s). This report is crucial for understanding your business's financial stability and its ability to meet obligations.

Key parts of a Balance Sheet:

- **Assets:** These are things your business owns that have value. Assets can be:
    - *Current Assets:* Items like cash, accounts receivable, and inventory that are expected to be used or converted into cash within a year.
    - *Fixed Assets:* Long-term resources such as property, equipment, and vehicles that are used to run your business.
- **Liabilities:** These are debts or obligations your business owes. Liabilities include:
    - *Current Liabilities:* Debts due within a year, like accounts payable, wages, and taxes.
    - *Long-term Liabilities:* Debts that will be paid over a longer time, such as loans or mortgages.
- **Equity:** This is what's left for the owner(s) after subtracting liabilities from assets. It includes retained earnings and money invested by the owner(s).

The Balance Sheet helps you determine if your business has enough resources to pay its short-term bills and manage long-term stability. For instance, comparing your current assets to your current liabilities can reveal whether you have enough cash flow to cover immediate expenses. Reviewing this report ensures that your business remains financially healthy and prepared for growth.

The Statement of Owner's Equity

The Statement of Owner's Equity, also called the Statement of Changes in Equity, shows how the owner's share in the business changes over a specific period. It's particularly useful for sole proprietors and partnerships to track how profits, investments, and withdrawals affect ownership.

Key parts of the Statement of Owner's Equity:

- **Beginning Equity:** The amount of equity at the start of the period.

- **Additions to Equity:** Includes net profits earned and any extra capital contributed by the owner(s) during the period.

- **Deductions from Equity:** Covers money withdrawn by the owner(s) and any losses incurred by the business.

- **Ending Equity:** This is calculated by adding Beginning Equity and Additions, then subtracting Deductions. It shows the updated equity balance at the end of the period.

This report complements the Balance Sheet by explaining changes in equity and helping you understand how owner-related activities, such as withdrawing funds for personal use, impact the overall financial position of your business. It's also useful for preparing taxes and planning for future investments.

Why These Reports Matter

Each of these reports gives you a unique view of your business's finances:

- The P&L shows how profitable your business is over time, helping you see where you can improve and make smarter spending decisions.

- The Balance Sheet shows whether your business is stable and has enough resources to cover debts and invest in future growth.

- The Statement of Owner's Equity shows how profits, investments, and withdrawals affect the owner's share in the business.

Understanding these reports helps you make better decisions for your business. For example, if your P&L shows a drop in profit, you might review your expenses or adjust pricing. If your Balance Sheet shows high liabilities compared to assets, it could mean you need to improve cash flow or reduce debt. These reports are also critical when working with banks or investors who want to see how financially sound your business is.

By reviewing these financial reports regularly, you can stay ahead of challenges, take advantage of new opportunities, and ensure your business grows steadily. They are your roadmap to building a successful, sustainable business that thrives in the years to come.

Section 2: How to Generate These Reports Using Software

Creating financial reports like Profit and Loss (P&L) statements and Balance Sheets is much easier with bookkeeping software. While there are lots of good options, this section will focus on QuickBooks because it is the most popular choice for small businesses. QuickBooks is well-known for its easy-to-use features and its ability to provide accurate financial information, which makes it a great tool for small business owners.

1. Pick Your Software

QuickBooks is one of the best accounting tools for small businesses. It helps you create reports by handling the calculations, organizing your transactions, and formatting your data so it looks professional. Other tools, like Xero, Wave, and FreshBooks, work well too, but QuickBooks is the most widely used and has the best support. If you use another program, make sure it offers the same important features, like customizable reports and connections to your other systems.

2. Enter and Organize Your Data

Before you can create accurate reports, you need to make sure all your financial data is entered and organized in QuickBooks. Getting this step right is very important. Here's what you need to do:

- **Record Your Transactions:** Add all your income and expense transactions to QuickBooks regularly. You can use bank feeds to automatically import these transactions, which saves time and reduces errors.

- **Categorize Transactions:** Put each transaction into the correct account in your Chart of Accounts. This will make sure your reports show the right information about your business.

- **Reconcile Accounts:** Check that your bank and credit card accounts match the records in QuickBooks. Fix any differences to make sure all your information is correct.

When you complete these steps, your data will be ready to generate accurate reports that give you a clear view of your business's finances.

3. Go to the Reports Section

To find the reports in QuickBooks, click the "Reports" tab in the main menu. This section is where you can create different financial statements, like P&L statements and Balance Sheets. The menu is easy to use and organizes reports by categories, like expenses, sales, and business overview. Take some time to explore this section so you can find the reports you need quickly.

4. Pick the Type of Report

Once you're in the reports section, choose the type of report you need. QuickBooks offers lots of options, but these two are the most important:

- **Profit and Loss Statement (Income Statement):** This report shows your income and expenses for a specific time period and helps you see if your business made a profit or loss.

- **Balance Sheet:** This report gives you a snapshot of your business's financial position at a specific time. It lists your assets, liabilities, and equity so you can see your overall financial health.

You can also check out other reports, like cash flow statements or sales summaries, depending on what information you need.

5. Customize Your Report

QuickBooks lets you change your reports to show exactly what you need. Here are some of the ways you can customize them:

- **Date Range:** Pick the time period you want to see, like this month, last quarter, or year-to-date.
- **Comparison Periods:** Compare how your business did in different time periods to spot trends or seasonal changes.
- **Accounts:** Choose which accounts to include in the report to focus on the most important details.
- **Formatting:** Adjust how the data looks by grouping items together, showing percentages, or adding transaction details.

Customizing your report makes it easier to understand and more useful for your goals.

6. Generate the Report

Once your settings are ready, click the "Run Report" button. QuickBooks will use your data to create the report. The report is interactive, so you can click on numbers to see the transactions behind them. This feature is helpful if you need to investigate anything unusual or get more details.

7. Review and Share Your Report

After the report is created, review it carefully to make sure everything is correct. Here's what to look for:

- **Fix Errors:** Check for anything unusual, like uncategorized transactions, strange balances, or missing data. Fix these issues to make sure your report is accurate.

- **Understand the Data:** Look for patterns or problem areas. For example, a P&L statement might show which products are not selling well or where expenses are too high.

When the report looks good, you can:

- **Export the Report:** Save it as a PDF or Excel file so you can share it with others or keep it for your records.

- **Print the Report:** Print a hard copy for meetings, audits, or presentations. Having a printed version is also handy for quick reference.

Tips for Using QuickBooks Effectively

- **Automate Tasks:** Use features like bank feeds and recurring transactions to save time and reduce mistakes.

- **Set Up Scheduled Reports:** QuickBooks can automatically create and send you regular reports. This keeps you updated without extra work.

- **Learn More Features:** QuickBooks offers tools like budgeting, forecasting, and payroll integration. Using these can give you a more complete view of your finances.

- **Use Support Tools:** QuickBooks has tutorials, webinars, and forums to help you learn and solve problems. Take advantage of these resources to become more confident with the software.

By using QuickBooks and following these steps, you can easily create professional financial reports that give you valuable insights into your business. These reports are not just for taxes—they're also important tools to help you make smart decisions and plan for the future.

Section 3: Understanding Financial Reports to Make Better Decisions

Once you've created your financial reports, the next step is to understand what they're telling you. These reports are like a guidebook for your business, showing what's working, what's not, and where you can make improvements. Let's break it down step by step.

1. Breaking Down the Profit and Loss (P&L) Statement

The Profit and Loss Statement, or P&L, shows how much money your business earned and spent over a certain time. Here's how to read it:

- **Revenue (Sales)**: Look at your total sales. Are they going up, going down, or staying the same? Are some products or services doing better than others? This helps you see where your money is coming from and what needs more attention.

- **Cost of Goods Sold (COGS)**: If you sell products, this is how much it costs to make or buy them. If this cost is too high compared to your sales, you might need to find cheaper materials or make your production process more efficient.

- **Gross Profit Margin**: This is what's left after subtracting COGS from your revenue. It tells you how good you are at making money from your products or services. If it's low, it might mean your costs are too high or your prices are too low.

- **Operating Expenses**: These are things like rent, utilities, payroll, and advertising. Are these costs reasonable compared to your sales? If they're too high, you might need to cut back or find ways to save.

- **Net Profit (Your Bottom Line)**: This is what's left after all expenses are paid. If this number is low or negative, it's a sign that changes are needed—either reducing costs or boosting sales.

2. Understanding the Balance Sheet

The Balance Sheet shows what your business owns, what it owes, and the overall value of the business at a specific point in time. Here's what to look for:

- **Assets**: These are things your business owns, like cash, accounts receivable (money customers owe you), inventory, equipment, or property. Are these enough to support your business and pay your bills? For example, too much inventory could mean you're overstocked.

- **Liabilities**: These are debts your business owes, like loans, accounts payable (bills you owe), or taxes. Compare these to your assets. If your liabilities are much higher than your assets, it could be a warning sign that you need to reduce debt or slow down spending.

- **Equity**: This is what's left after subtracting liabilities from assets. It's the value of the business that belongs to you, the owner. A positive number means the business is financially healthy, while a negative number might mean you need to improve your finances.

3. What the Statement of Owner's Equity Tells You

The Statement of Owner's Equity explains how the value of your business has changed over time. It ties together the P&L and Balance Sheet. Pay attention to these parts:

- **Starting Equity**: This is the value of the business at the beginning of the time period.
- **Owner Contributions**: Money or assets you've added to the business during the period.
- **Net Income or Loss**: This comes from the P&L. If your business made a profit, this adds to your equity. If it lost money, your equity goes down.
- **Owner Withdrawals**: Any money or assets you took out of the business for personal use. This reduces equity.
- **Ending Equity**: The value of the business at the end of the period. If it's growing over time, your business is likely on the right track.

4. Using Ratios to Dig Deeper

Ratios are tools that help you understand your reports better. Here are a few simple ones to use:

- **Current Ratio**: Current Assets ÷ Current Liabilities. If the number is above 1, it means you can pay your short-term bills.

- **Debt-to-Equity Ratio**: Total Liabilities ÷ Owner's Equity. A high number means you're relying heavily on debt, which can be risky.

- **Gross Margin**: Gross Profit ÷ Revenue. This shows how much money you keep from each sale after covering product costs.

- **Net Profit Margin**: Net Profit ÷ Revenue. This tells you how much of each dollar you earn turns into profit.

- **Return on Equity (ROE)**: Net Income ÷ Average Owner's Equity. This shows how well your business is using the owner's investment to make money.

5. Connecting the Dots Between Reports

Each report tells part of the story, but together they give the full picture. For example:

- If your P&L shows strong sales but low profit, check the operating expenses to see if they're too high.

- If your Balance Sheet shows low cash, look at accounts receivable to see if customers are paying on time.

- If your Statement of Owner's Equity shows large withdrawals, make sure your profits are enough to support that.

By looking at how these reports work together, you can figure out where your business is doing well and where you need to improve.

6. Using This Information to Make Decisions

Once you've understood your reports, use them to guide your next steps. For example:

- **Pricing**: If your profit margin is low, you might need to raise prices or cut costs.
- **Expenses**: Look for areas where you're spending too much, like utilities or supplies, and find ways to reduce costs.
- **Growth Plans**: If your reports show consistent profit and growing equity, it might be time to invest in marketing, hire more staff, or expand your business.
- **Cash Flow**: If cash is tight, focus on collecting payments faster or negotiating better terms with suppliers.

7. Review Regularly and Adapt

Financial reports aren't just for tax time—they're tools you should use all year. Check them monthly or quarterly to see how your business is doing. Over time, you'll notice patterns, like which months are slower or where costs tend to creep up. Use this information to set realistic goals and make smarter decisions.

By regularly reviewing your Profit and Loss Statement, Balance Sheet, and Statement of Owner's Equity, you'll stay in control of your business's finances. These reports help you spot problems early, plan for growth, and make decisions that keep your business moving forward.

Chapter 8: How Can I Ensure My Books Are Accurate and Up-to-Date?

Section 1: Common Bookkeeping Mistakes to Avoid

Bookkeeping is a key part of running your small business, but even experienced business owners can slip up. Knowing about common mistakes and learning how to avoid them can save you time, reduce stress, and make sure your financial records are accurate. Understanding these errors in detail can help you prevent them and build a stronger financial foundation for your business. Let's explore some frequent bookkeeping mistakes, why they happen, and how to avoid them effectively.

1. Mixing Personal and Business Finances

Many small business owners make the mistake of mixing their personal and business expenses. When you combine these accounts, it becomes harder to keep track of what belongs to your business, which can cause confusion during tax season and make it difficult to understand how well your business is actually doing.

Why It Happens:

- Convenience of using one account for all expenses.
- Lack of knowledge about how to separate finances effectively.

How to Avoid:

- Open a separate bank account and credit card solely for business use. This creates a clear boundary between personal and business finances.

- Use bookkeeping software that helps you easily categorize transactions as personal or business-related.

- Schedule regular reviews of your financial records to catch and correct any mix-ups promptly.

2. Failing to Track All Expenses

Small expenses might not seem significant, but over time, they add up. If you forget to record these costs, your financial records can become incomplete. This can lead to inaccurate budgeting and missed tax deductions, costing you money in the long run.

Why It Happens:

- Small cash purchases are easy to forget.

- Lack of a system for tracking receipts and transactions.

How to Avoid:

- Always save receipts, whether they're paper or digital. Tools like receipt-scanning apps can make this process easier.

- Use software that lets you log expenses immediately, even from your smartphone.
- Make it a habit to review your expenses daily or weekly to ensure everything is accounted for.

3. Not Reconciling Bank Accounts Regularly

When you don't reconcile your bank accounts often, your records might not match your actual bank balances. This can lead to overdrafts, missed payments, and financial reports that don't reflect reality.

Why It Happens:

- Business owners may feel too busy to reconcile accounts frequently.
- A lack of understanding about how to perform reconciliations.

How to Avoid:

- Reconcile your accounts at least once a month, or ideally weekly, to ensure your records align with your bank statements.
- Leverage bookkeeping software that automates reconciliation by matching transactions with bank records.
- Set calendar reminders to complete this task regularly.

4. Misclassifying Transactions

If you categorize income or expenses incorrectly, your financial reports might not provide an accurate picture of your business's performance. This can also lead to paying more taxes than necessary or missing important deductions.

Why It Happens:

- Unfamiliarity with the Chart of Accounts.
- Lack of attention to detail when categorizing transactions.

How to Avoid:

- Take time to understand the Chart of Accounts and how it applies to your business.
- Update your categories as your business grows or changes, ensuring they stay relevant.
- When unsure, consult with a bookkeeper or accountant to double-check your classifications.

5. Overlooking Sales Tax Obligations

If your business sells products or services that require sales tax, forgetting to collect or remit it can lead to fines, penalties, and unnecessary stress.

Why It Happens:

- Not knowing local or state sales tax rules.
- Lack of systems to track and manage sales tax.

How to Avoid:

- Research the sales tax rules in your area, including any changes that may affect your business.

- Set up bookkeeping software to automatically calculate, track, and report sales tax.
- Review your sales tax payments regularly to ensure compliance with local laws.

6. Neglecting to Back Up Financial Records

Losing important financial data due to a computer crash, theft, or natural disaster can be devastating. Without backups, you risk losing months or years of vital information.

Why It Happens:

- Overreliance on physical records or local storage.
- Lack of awareness about backup options.

How to Avoid:

- Use cloud-based accounting software that automatically backs up your data in real-time.
- Keep physical copies of critical documents, such as tax filings, in a secure location like a fireproof safe.
- Regularly test your backup systems to ensure they're working correctly and covering all essential data.

7. Delaying Bookkeeping Tasks

Procrastinating on bookkeeping tasks can lead to rushed work, overlooked details, and errors. The longer you delay, the more overwhelming the backlog becomes, making it harder to ensure accuracy.

Why It Happens:

- Feeling too busy or prioritizing other tasks.
- Not having a set schedule for bookkeeping.

How to Avoid:

- Dedicate specific times each week to update your books and review transactions.
- Automate repetitive tasks like invoicing and bill payments to save time.
- Use checklists to track essential bookkeeping tasks and mark them off as you go.

8. Ignoring Financial Reports

Financial reports like profit and loss statements, balance sheets, and cash flow statements are essential for understanding your business's health. Ignoring these reports can lead to missed opportunities and a lack of awareness about potential problems.

Why It Happens:

- Not understanding how to interpret financial reports.
- Underestimating their importance for decision-making.

How to Avoid:

- Make it a habit to review your financial reports monthly. Look for patterns, trends, and areas that need attention.

- Partner with an accountant or bookkeeper who can help you analyze the data and explain what it means for your business.
- Use the insights from your reports to set goals, adjust your budget, and plan for the future.

By avoiding these common bookkeeping mistakes and taking proactive steps, you can keep your records accurate and up-to-date. This will help you run your business more smoothly, reduce financial stress, and give you the tools you need to make informed decisions.

Section 2: Tips for Keeping Bookkeeping Accurate

Keeping accurate books is very important for the success and health of your business. Bad or outdated records can cause big problems, like mistakes, tax penalties, and lost chances to save money. Here are simple tips, explained clearly, to help you keep your bookkeeping correct:

1. Keep Personal and Business Finances Separate

Many small business owners make the mistake of mixing personal and business finances. Open a separate bank account for your business and use a different credit card for business expenses. Keeping them separate makes it easier to track spending and avoid mistakes. It also helps you with taxes and protects you legally by showing your business is its own entity.

2. Use Easy-to-Use Bookkeeping Software

Get good bookkeeping software, like QuickBooks, Xero, or Wave. These programs help you calculate numbers, make financial reports, and avoid human errors. Many of these tools can automatically categorize expenses, link with your bank, and give you real-time updates. Always update your software to use new features and stay secure.

3. Record Transactions Every Day

Don't wait to log your transactions. Spend time each day recording income, expenses, and other financial actions. Doing this daily prevents you from forgetting details and helps keep your books current. Daily tracking can also help you notice trends, watch cash flow, and catch any suspicious activity.

4. Reconcile Bank and Credit Card Accounts Often

Reconciliation means comparing your bank and credit card statements with your bookkeeping records to find any mistakes. Do this at least once a month, but weekly is better if your business has a lot of transactions. This helps you spot problems, like errors or unauthorized charges, early on.

5. Organize Expenses Clearly

Have a clear system for categorizing expenses. Use a Chart of Accounts to organize them into logical groups. Avoid using vague categories like "miscellaneous" since they can cause confusion. Update your categories as your business grows to keep them helpful and accurate.

6. Use Checks and Balances

If someone else helps with your bookkeeping, make sure there are checks and balances. For example, have one person handle invoices and another manage payments to lower the chance of mistakes or fraud. Regularly review their work to make sure it's correct, and set up approvals for big transactions.

7. Save All Your Receipts and Documents

Keep receipts, invoices, and any other paperwork for all transactions. Use apps or scanners to save these documents digitally. These records prove your financial entries are correct and can help during audits. Organize them by month or type to make them easy to find later.

8. Learn About Tax and Finance Rules

Tax and finance rules change often. Stay up to date so you don't accidentally break any laws. Talk to a tax expert or bookkeeper if you're unsure. Signing up for newsletters or attending workshops can also keep you informed.

9. Audit Your Books Regularly

Plan regular checks of your financial records. This can be a quick review every quarter or a deeper audit with an outside expert. Audits catch mistakes or problems before they get worse. They also help you find ways to save time or money.

10. Ask for Help if Needed

If bookkeeping feels too hard or takes up too much time, hire a bookkeeper or accountant. They can fix errors, improve your system, and save you time so you can focus on running your business. Experts make sure your books are accurate and ready for taxes.

11. Stick to a Bookkeeping Routine

Make a schedule for your bookkeeping tasks. Set aside time each week or month to enter transactions, check accounts, and review reports. A regular routine keeps you organized and prevents last-minute scrambling.

12. Use Automation Tools

Automation can save you time and reduce errors. Many software programs let you set up automatic bank connections, recurring invoices, and expense categories. These features make your bookkeeping process smoother and more accurate.

By following these tips and staying proactive, you can keep your financial records accurate and up to date. Good bookkeeping isn't just about staying out of trouble with taxes; it also helps your business grow and succeed.

Section 3: Setting Up a Bookkeeping Schedule

Having a regular bookkeeping schedule is essential for keeping your financial records accurate and making smart business decisions. When you dedicate consistent time to updating and reviewing your books, you can catch mistakes, reduce stress during tax season, and gain a clearer understanding of your business's financial health. A well-organized schedule not only keeps you on track but also ensures long-term success. Here's how to create and stick to a bookkeeping schedule that works for you:

1. Decide How Often to Do Tasks

Breaking your bookkeeping responsibilities into smaller, regular tasks can make them easier to manage and less overwhelming. Here's a breakdown of common bookkeeping tasks and how often you should complete them:

- **Daily Tasks:**
    - Record sales and income: Keep track of all sales, whether they come from cash, card, or online payments. This keeps your income records current and accurate.
    - Log expenses: Document every expense, such as supplies, utilities, or travel costs, to ensure you don't miss any deductions.
    - Monitor cash flow: Check how much money is coming in and going out to ensure you have enough cash for daily operations and unexpected expenses.
- **Weekly Tasks:**
    - Reconcile transactions: Match your bank and credit card transactions with your

records to identify and fix discrepancies quickly.

- o Pay bills: Schedule payments for suppliers, utilities, or subscriptions to avoid late fees and maintain good relationships.

- o Send invoices: Create and issue invoices to customers. Follow up on overdue payments to keep your cash flow steady.

- o Review accounts payable and receivable: Monitor what you owe and what others owe you to avoid falling behind on payments or collections.

- **Monthly Tasks:**

  - o Reconcile accounts: Compare your books to your bank and credit card statements to confirm accuracy.

  - o Generate financial reports: Review profit and loss statements, balance sheets, and cash flow reports to understand your business's performance.

  - o Check inventory: Verify that your inventory records match the actual stock on hand to prevent overstocking or shortages.

  - o Allocate funds for taxes: Set aside money for estimated taxes to avoid scrambling when payments are due.

- **Quarterly Tasks:**
    - File estimated taxes: Submit your quarterly tax payments based on your earnings for the past three months.
    - Evaluate progress: Review your financial goals and performance, and make adjustments as needed.
    - Meet with an advisor: Schedule a meeting with your bookkeeper or accountant to get professional insights and advice.
- **Annual Tasks:**
    - Prepare and file taxes: Gather all necessary documents and ensure your filings are accurate and complete.
    - Review yearly performance: Analyze your business's financial health over the year and identify areas for improvement.
    - Set goals for the next year: Develop a plan for growth, including budgets and financial strategies.

2. Pick Specific Days and Times

Consistency is key to an effective bookkeeping schedule. Assign specific days and times for tasks to make them a regular part of your routine. For example:

- Record daily transactions at the end of each business day to ensure accuracy while the details are still fresh in your mind.

- Reserve Friday afternoons to reconcile accounts, review the week's finances, and prepare for the upcoming week.
- Use the first Monday of each month to analyze financial reports and assess monthly performance.
- Schedule quarterly reviews during the first week of each new quarter to keep your financial plans on track.

By dedicating time to these tasks, you'll reduce the risk of errors and avoid falling behind.

3. Use Technology to Save Time

Bookkeeping software can simplify your workflow and improve accuracy. Tools like QuickBooks, Xero, and Wave offer features that make bookkeeping easier, including:

- **Automatic Transaction Import:** Connect your bank and credit card accounts to automatically import transactions, reducing manual data entry.
- **Recurring Invoices and Payments:** Set up automated schedules for regular invoices and bill payments.
- **Reminders and Alerts:** Get notifications for overdue invoices, upcoming bill deadlines, and other important tasks.

- **Quick Reports:** Generate detailed financial reports with just a few clicks to save time and gain insights.

These tools can significantly cut down the time you spend on bookkeeping, allowing you to focus on growing your business.

4. Adjust Your Schedule When Needed

Your bookkeeping schedule should adapt to changes in your business. Regularly evaluate its effectiveness by asking yourself:

- Are tasks being completed on time?
- Is the schedule manageable, or do certain tasks need to be rescheduled?
- Are you using the best tools and processes for your current needs?

For example, a small business with limited transactions might only need weekly updates, while a larger operation might require daily attention. Stay flexible and adjust your schedule as your business evolves.

5. Consider Outsourcing When Necessary

If keeping up with bookkeeping becomes overwhelming, it may be time to hire help. Professional bookkeepers or accountants can:

- Handle complex tasks like tax preparation, audits, or payroll.

- Ensure compliance with financial regulations and legal requirements.
- Offer valuable advice for financial planning and decision-making.

Outsourcing allows you to focus on running your business while ensuring your financial records are accurate and up-to-date.

6. Stick to the Schedule

The most important part of any bookkeeping schedule is following through. Treat bookkeeping as a priority, not an afterthought. Use tools like calendar reminders or task management apps to stay on track. When you consistently follow your schedule, you'll:

- Avoid costly errors and missed deadlines.
- Gain a clearer picture of your financial health.
- Be better prepared for audits, tax filings, or big financial decisions.

A reliable bookkeeping schedule lays the foundation for your business's success. Whether you're just starting or managing a growing company, putting in the effort now will save you time and stress later. Take control of your finances today to build a stronger, more stable future for your business.

Chapter 9: What Records Should I Keep, and For How Long?

Section 1: Types of Records (Invoices, Receipts, Contracts)

Keeping accurate and detailed records is essential for your small business. Records help you manage finances, comply with legal requirements, and be prepared for audits or reviews. They also provide insights that can guide better decisions for your business. Below, we'll cover the main types of records you should maintain, why they matter, and how to organize them effectively.

1. Invoices

Invoices serve as documentation for the sales and services your business provides. They are vital for tracking revenue, managing customer payments, and maintaining accurate financial records. Be sure to keep both digital and paper copies of:

- **Customer invoices**: These documents detail the products or services sold, including dates, amounts, payment terms, and customer details. They help you track income, follow up on overdue payments, and resolve any disputes quickly.

- **Vendor invoices**: These show what your business has purchased from suppliers or contractors. They are essential for managing accounts payable and ensuring that your expenses align with your budget.

Organized invoices allow you to stay on top of financial obligations and give you a clear picture of your cash flow.

2. Receipts

Receipts are crucial for documenting expenses and are often required for tax deductions. Keeping detailed receipts helps you monitor spending and ensures you're prepared in case of an audit. Common types of receipts to save include:

- **Office supplies and equipment**: Purchases like desks, computers, and tools that support your operations.

- **Utility bills**: Expenses such as electricity, internet, and phone services that keep your business running.

- **Travel and lodging**: Costs for business-related trips, including airfare, hotel stays, and transportation.

- **Meals and entertainment**: If these expenses are related to client meetings or team events, they might be tax-deductible.

- **Recurring costs**: Subscriptions or memberships, such as software licenses or professional organizations, that recur monthly or annually.

Ensure receipts include the date, amount paid, vendor, and a brief description of the purchase. This makes them easier to categorize and use for both accounting and tax purposes.

3. Contracts and Agreements

Contracts are formal agreements that protect your business and clarify the expectations of both parties. They are essential for reducing risks and resolving disputes. Examples of contracts to keep include:

- **Client agreements**: These outline the scope of work, deliverables, payment terms, and deadlines for projects.

- **Employment contracts**: These specify the roles, responsibilities, pay, and benefits of employees.

- **Supplier agreements**: These detail the terms under which goods or services are provided to your business.

- **Lease agreements**: Documentation for renting office space, equipment, or vehicles.

Storing contracts in a well-organized system allows for easy access when you need to review terms or resolve conflicts.

4. Bank and Credit Card Statements

Bank and credit card statements provide a clear view of your business's financial transactions. They are essential for reconciling accounts, spotting fraud, and understanding your spending patterns. Be sure to:

- Review statements monthly to ensure all transactions are accurate.

- Save statements as part of your financial records for tax preparation and audits.

These records offer a detailed snapshot of cash flow and can help you identify opportunities to cut costs or improve profitability.

5. Tax Records

Tax records ensure compliance with regulations and make filing taxes easier. Proper documentation can also protect you during an audit. Key tax records to maintain include:

- **Filed tax returns**: Keep copies of returns for at least seven years.
- **Income records**: This includes invoices, receipts, and bank deposit records.
- **Expense records**: Proof of deductions, such as receipts and bills.
- **Payroll tax records**: If you have employees, retain records of taxes withheld and paid.

Organizing these records throughout the year simplifies tax filing and minimizes stress during deadlines.

6. Employee Records

If your business has employees, maintaining detailed employee records is both a legal requirement and a practical necessity. Examples include:

- **Timecards and attendance records**: These help ensure accurate payroll calculations.

- **Pay stubs and payroll records**: These document payments to employees and are needed for tax reporting.
- **Benefits enrollment forms**: Records of employees participating in health insurance, retirement plans, or other benefits.
- **Performance reviews and disciplinary records**: These provide a history of employee achievements and any workplace issues.

Organized employee records help you manage your team effectively and stay compliant with labor laws.

7. Licenses and Permits

Maintaining up-to-date licenses and permits ensures that your business operates legally. Examples include:

- Industry-specific licenses
- Zoning permits
- Sales tax permits

Store these documents securely and renew them as required to avoid interruptions in business operations.

8. Insurance Policies

Insurance protects your business from risks and liabilities. Important insurance records to keep include:

- **Liability insurance**: Covers claims or lawsuits.
- **Property insurance**: Protects your physical assets, such as office buildings or equipment.

- **Worker's compensation**: Required in most states for businesses with employees.

Save documentation for all policies, claims filed, and any correspondence with your insurer to ensure easy access when needed.

9. Asset Records

Keep detailed records of the assets your business owns. These are useful for taxes, planning, and securing loans. Examples include:

- **Purchase invoices**: For equipment, machinery, or other major purchases.

- **Depreciation schedules**: Showing how asset values decrease over time.

- **Titles or deeds**: For vehicles or property owned by the business.

These records are valuable for determining the worth of your business and planning for future investments or sales.

10. Miscellaneous Documents

Every business has unique needs, so you might need additional records depending on your industry. Examples include:

- **Intellectual property filings**: Such as trademarks, patents, or copyrights.

- **Compliance records**: Proof that you follow industry regulations or standards.
- **Customer feedback and surveys**: Useful for improving your products or services.

By keeping all your records well-organized, you can run your business more efficiently, stay legally compliant, and be prepared for any challenges or opportunities that arise.

Section 2: Organizing Records for Easy Access

Keeping your business records organized is essential for smooth operations. Whether it's for tax preparation, loan applications, or audits, having a clear system will save time, reduce stress, and ensure your business is always prepared. In this section, we'll guide you through setting up an effective system for managing your records, from choosing the right tools to creating habits that keep everything in order.

1. Choose the Right Filing System

The first step to staying organized is deciding how to store your records. Your filing system can be physical, digital, or a mix of both. Whichever method you choose, make sure it is easy to follow and consistent.

- **Physical Filing Systems**: For paper records, use labeled folders, binders, or accordion files to group similar documents, such as receipts, invoices, and contracts. Organize these by category, then further sort them by date, client, or project. Store these files in filing cabinets or fireproof boxes to protect them from damage. If space is a concern, consider off-site storage for older, archived records.

- **Digital Filing Systems**: Digital systems are ideal for businesses that want quick, remote access to records. Create folders on your computer or in a cloud storage system like Google Drive, Dropbox, or OneDrive. Organize these folders by broad categories like "Taxes," "Invoices," or "Payroll" and use subfolders to sort by year, month, or project. For example:
  - Main folder: **"Taxes"**
  - Subfolders: **"2023_Q1", "2023_Q2"**, etc.

Digital filing not only saves space but also allows you to use search functions to find specific documents quickly.

- **Combination Systems**: If you need to keep original signed documents but want the convenience of digital access, use a hybrid system. Scan important papers and save them electronically while keeping the physical copies stored securely.

2. Use Technology to Simplify Record Keeping

Technology can make managing your records faster and more efficient. Take advantage of tools that automate or streamline parts of the process:

- **Accounting Software**: Platforms like QuickBooks, Xero, or FreshBooks let you upload and categorize receipts, invoices, and other documents. These programs often integrate with your bank accounts and credit cards, automatically matching transactions to their related documents.

- **Document Scanning Apps**: Apps like Adobe Scan, CamScanner, or Microsoft Lens allow you to scan physical documents directly into digital formats. Many of these apps have Optical Character Recognition (OCR), which makes scanned files searchable by keyword.

- **Expense Tracking Tools**: Apps like Expensify or Dext let you take photos of receipts, categorize them, and save them to your accounting system. This is especially useful for businesses with a lot of small transactions.

- **Cloud Storage Solutions**: Services like Google Drive or Dropbox allow you to store, share, and access files securely from anywhere. They also provide automatic backup options to protect your data in case of computer failures.

By combining these tools, you can build a system that minimizes manual work and ensures your records are always accessible.

3. Develop a Clear Naming System

An organized filing system needs clear and consistent file names. When naming files, include details like the document type, date, and client or vendor name. This makes it easy to identify the document at a glance. For example:

- **Invoices**: [Client Name]*[Invoice Number]*[Date]
    - Example: SmithCo_Invoice001_2024-01-15.pdf
- **Receipts**: [Vendor Name]*[Expense Type]*[Date]
    - Example: Staples_OfficeSupplies_2024-01-10.jpg
- **Contracts**: [Client Name]*Contract*[Start Date-End Date]
    - Example: JohnsonCorp_Contract_2024-2025.pdf

Having a consistent naming system also allows you to use search functions effectively, especially for digital records.

4. Create and Maintain a Records Index

A records index acts like a map of your filing system. It lists the categories of records you keep, where they are stored, and how long you plan to keep them. For example:

Category	Subcategory	Storage Location	Retention Period
Invoices	2024 Invoices	Digital Folder "Invoices"	7 Years
Payroll Records	Q1 2024 Pay Stubs	Filing Cabinet A, Drawer 2	3 Years
Contracts	Client ABC, 2024-2025	Cloud Folder "Contracts"	Permanent

Update this index whenever you add or move files. It will save you time when searching for specific documents.

5. Build Regular Habits

Keeping your records organized requires regular effort. Build habits into your schedule to ensure everything stays in order:

- **Weekly Tasks**:
    - File new receipts, invoices, and other documents.

- o Scan physical records and upload them to your digital system.

- **Monthly Tasks**:
    - o Reconcile your financial records with your bank statements.
    - o Check that all documents are filed in the correct folders and categories.

- **Yearly Tasks**:
    - o Review your entire filing system to ensure it's still working for your needs.
    - o Move older records to an archive or off-site storage.
    - o Safely dispose of records that are no longer needed and are past their legal retention period.

6. Protect Your Records

Your records contain sensitive information, so keeping them secure is a priority. Here's how to protect them:

- **Physical Records**: Use fireproof and waterproof storage for critical paper files. Keep these in a secure location, such as a locked cabinet, to prevent unauthorized access.

- **Digital Records**: Use strong passwords and enable two-factor authentication for access to your files. Back up your digital records regularly to an external hard drive or a secure cloud service. Encrypt sensitive files for an added layer of security.

7. Color-Code and Categorize

Adding visual aids like colors or tags can make it easier to locate records quickly. For example:

- Use blue folders for payroll records, green for tax-related documents, and red for contracts.
- In digital systems, you can tag files or folders with colors or labels to group similar items.

8. Train Your Team

If you have employees or partners helping with record-keeping, make sure they understand the system. Provide training on how to:

- File and categorize documents.
- Use the tools and software you've chosen.
- Follow security protocols for sensitive information.

Clear guidelines ensure everyone is on the same page, reducing errors and misplaced records.

9. Archive Older Records

To prevent your filing system from becoming cluttered, move older records into an archive. Label archived files with their retention periods and store them separately. For example:

- Create a separate cloud folder or external hard drive for digital archives.
- Use labeled boxes or cabinets for physical files that don't need frequent access.

Review archived records yearly and dispose of any that are no longer required.

10. Stay Audit-Ready

A well-organized system ensures you're always prepared for audits or compliance checks. Regularly review your records to make sure you have all the documents you might need. Many accounting tools include audit trail features, which track changes and help confirm your records are accurate.

By following these steps, you'll create a system that's easy to maintain and works for your business's needs. Organized records save time, reduce stress, and help your business appear professional and reliable. With this foundation, you'll always be prepared for whatever comes your way.

PART II: TAXES

Chapter 10: What are the Benefits of Setting Up My Business as a Sole Proprietorship, Partnership, LLC, S-Corp, or C-Corp?

Section 1: Overview of Business Structures

When you start or grow a small business, one of the first important decisions you'll need to make is choosing a business structure. This choice affects your taxes, your personal responsibility for business debts, how your business runs day to day, and even your long-term goals like expanding or bringing in investors. It's important to understand the different options so you can choose what's best for you. Below is a detailed explanation of the most common business structures in the United States: sole proprietorship, partnership, limited liability company (LLC), S corporation (S-Corp), and C corporation (C-Corp).

Sole Proprietorship

A sole proprietorship is the simplest way to set up a business. It's run by one person, and there's no legal separation between the business and the owner. This means the owner is responsible for all the business's debts and legal problems.

Key Features:

- Very easy and cheap to set up—you might just need a local business license.
- Few rules and regulations to follow.
- The owner handles business income and expenses on their personal tax return.

- Full control over all business decisions.

Advantages:

- Perfect for small operations with low financial risk.
- No need for complicated paperwork or formal meetings.
- Allows for fast decision-making since the owner has full control.

Challenges:

- The owner is personally responsible for all debts and legal issues.
- Hard to raise money since you can't sell stock or attract investors.
- Business lifespan is tied to the owner's involvement.

Best For:

- Freelancers, consultants, small-scale service providers, and home-based businesses.

Partnership

A partnership is when two or more people or businesses share ownership. There are general partnerships, where everyone shares responsibility, and limited partnerships, where some partners have less responsibility and liability.

Key Features:

- Easy to set up with a written agreement outlining everyone's roles and profit-sharing.
- Partners report profits and losses on their personal tax returns.
- Everyone shares decision-making and brings different skills and resources.

Advantages:

- Combines the talents, resources, and expertise of multiple people.
- Flexibility in how responsibilities and profits are shared.
- Can lead to faster business growth by pooling funds and efforts.

Challenges:

- Disagreements can happen over decisions or profit-sharing.
- General partners are personally responsible for the business's debts.
- Requires clear communication and a solid partnership agreement to avoid conflicts.

Best For:

- Small businesses with multiple founders, like law firms, creative agencies, or family businesses.

Limited Liability Company (LLC)

An LLC gives you the protection of a corporation but is easier to run and more flexible. It's a popular choice for small and medium-sized businesses.

Key Features:

- Protects personal assets from business debts and lawsuits.
- You can choose how it's taxed: like a sole proprietorship, partnership, or corporation.
- Fewer rules and less paperwork than corporations.
- Can have one owner (single-member LLC) or multiple owners (multi-member LLC).

Advantages:

- Personal assets are safe from most business risks.
- Flexible rules for managing the business and handling taxes.
- Suitable for many different industries and business sizes.
- Easier to attract investors compared to sole proprietorships or partnerships.

Challenges:

- Costs more to set up and maintain than a sole proprietorship.

- State-specific rules can complicate operating in multiple states.
- May involve extra fees, such as annual filing fees or franchise taxes.

Best For:

- Business owners who want liability protection without the complexity of corporations.

S Corporation (S-Corp)

An S-Corp is a type of corporation that lets profits and losses pass through to the owners' personal taxes. This avoids the "double taxation" of regular corporations, but there are more rules to follow.

Key Features:

- Can have up to 100 shareholders, all of whom must be U.S. citizens or residents.
- Business income is taxed at the owner level, not the corporate level.
- Shareholders must pay themselves a reasonable salary, which is subject to payroll taxes.

Advantages:

- Avoids double taxation while still offering liability protection.
- Can reduce overall tax burden with proper tax planning.

- Provides credibility and professionalism that may attract clients and investors.

Challenges:

- Strict rules about ownership and operations, such as limits on the number and type of shareholders.
- Requires more paperwork and formalities than an LLC.
- Must meet specific IRS requirements to maintain S-Corp status.

Best For:

- Small businesses looking for tax savings and liability protection, especially those with steady profits.

C Corporation (C-Corp)

A C-Corp is a separate legal entity from its owners. It offers the most protection and has the most potential for raising money, but it's also the most complicated.

Key Features:

- Can have an unlimited number of shareholders, including foreign investors.
- Can raise money by selling stock.
- Profits are taxed at the corporate level, and shareholders pay taxes on dividends (double taxation).

Advantages:

- Strong liability protection for shareholders.
- Best for businesses that want to grow quickly or go public.
- The company exists independently of its owners, so it can continue even if ownership changes.
- Easier to attract large-scale investors and venture capital funding.

Challenges:

- Expensive and complicated to set up and run, with strict regulatory requirements.
- Profits are taxed twice, reducing earnings.
- Requires a board of directors, corporate bylaws, and detailed record-keeping.

Best For:

- Large businesses, tech startups, or companies planning to seek significant investments or go public.

Picking the right structure takes careful thought about how you plan to run your business now and in the future. Each option has its own benefits and challenges, and your choice will influence your taxes, risk, and ability to grow. In the next sections, we'll dive deeper into how these structures impact taxes and provide tips for choosing the one that fits your goals best.

Section 2: Tax Implications for Each Structure

Picking the right business structure is important not just for how your business runs, but also for how much tax you'll pay. Understanding the details of how taxes work for each type of structure can help you avoid surprises and make the most cost-effective choice for your business. Here is an expanded breakdown of how taxes apply to each structure:

Sole Proprietorship

A sole proprietorship is the simplest type of business structure, but it comes with unique tax considerations:

- **Pass-through taxation:** The money your business makes is considered your personal income. This means your profits are reported directly on your personal tax return using Schedule C of Form 1040. Because there's no separate business tax return, this structure simplifies tax filing.

- **Self-employment tax:** As the owner, you are responsible for paying Social Security and Medicare taxes on your business profits, referred to as self-employment taxes. The rate is currently 15.3%, and it's calculated on your net income. Properly tracking expenses can reduce the amount of income subject to these taxes.

- **No separate business tax rates:** Since your business income is lumped together with your personal income, it could push you into a higher tax bracket. Making estimated quarterly tax payments is a must to avoid a large tax bill at the end of the year or potential penalties.

- **Limited deductions:** While you can claim business-related expenses, sole proprietors often miss out on some of the deductions available to other structures, such as health insurance costs for employees.

Partnership

Partnerships involve shared ownership, and taxes are handled differently than sole proprietorships:

- **Pass-through taxation:** Like sole proprietorships, partnerships do not pay taxes as a business. Instead, each partner reports their share of profits or losses on their personal tax return. These are detailed on a Schedule K-1 form provided by the partnership.

- **Self-employment tax:** Partners pay self-employment taxes on their share of the partnership's income, including guaranteed payments. This means that even if profits aren't distributed, partners might still owe taxes.

- **Additional tax forms:** The partnership must file an informational tax return (Form 1065) with the IRS. This shows the total income and how it's divided among the partners. While the partnership doesn't pay taxes directly, filing this return ensures transparency.

- **Flexibility in sharing profits:** Partnerships allow for flexibility in how profits and losses are divided, which can differ from ownership percentages. However, this flexibility requires well-documented agreements to avoid disputes.
- **Deductions for business expenses:** Partnerships can deduct expenses like rent, utilities, and supplies, reducing taxable income.

Limited Liability Company (LLC)

An LLC offers flexibility in taxation, giving owners (called members) more options:

- **Default pass-through taxation:** By default, single-member LLCs are taxed like sole proprietorships, and multi-member LLCs are taxed like partnerships. This means profits are passed directly to members' personal tax returns.
- **Option to be taxed as a corporation:** LLCs can choose to be taxed as either an S-Corp or a C-Corp by filing the appropriate IRS forms (Form 2553 for S-Corp or Form 8832 for C-Corp). This flexibility can save money depending on the business's size and profitability.
- **Self-employment tax:** Without electing a corporate tax status, LLC members pay self-employment taxes on their earnings. However, S-Corp status allows members to take part of their income as salary (subject to payroll taxes) and the rest as distributions (not subject to self-employment tax).

- **More deductions:** LLCs may have access to more deductions, such as retirement plan contributions and health insurance costs, making them attractive for small business owners.

S-Corporation (S-Corp)

S-Corps provide tax advantages for small businesses, but they come with rules to follow:

- **Pass-through taxation:** Similar to partnerships, S-Corps do not pay federal income tax at the corporate level. Instead, profits and losses are passed through to shareholders, who report them on their personal tax returns. This avoids double taxation.

- **Reasonable salaries for owners:** Shareholders who work for the business must pay themselves a reasonable salary, which is subject to payroll taxes. Any remaining profits can be distributed as dividends, which are not subject to self-employment tax. This structure can save significant tax dollars.

- **Extra tax forms:** S-Corps must file Form 1120-S annually and comply with rules like having no more than 100 shareholders, all of whom must be U.S. citizens or residents.

- **Strict eligibility rules:** S-Corps have strict rules, including only allowing one class of stock. Violating these rules can lead to the loss of S-Corp status.

- **Tax planning opportunities:** By carefully balancing salaries and dividends, S-Corps can reduce overall tax liability, but planning must follow IRS guidelines to avoid penalties.

C-Corporation (C-Corp)

C-Corps are taxed as separate entities, making them unique compared to other structures:

- **Double taxation:** A C-Corp pays taxes on its profits at the corporate level. When dividends are distributed to shareholders, they are taxed again at the individual level. This can make C-Corps less appealing to small businesses with regular profit distributions.

- **Flat corporate tax rate:** C-Corps pay a flat federal tax rate of 21%, which can be beneficial for businesses that reinvest most of their profits instead of distributing them as dividends.

- **Deductions for benefits:** C-Corps can deduct the cost of employee benefits like health insurance and retirement plans. This can make them attractive to businesses with many employees.

- **Complex tax filings:** C-Corps must file Form 1120 annually and meet stringent compliance requirements. Professional accounting services are often necessary to handle these complexities.

- **Ideal for growth:** C-Corps are well-suited for businesses planning to attract investors or go public, as they allow unlimited shareholders and easier access to capital markets.

Understanding how taxes work for each type of business can help you make the best decision for your goals. Be sure to consider legal and administrative factors as well. Consulting a tax professional or accountant can provide tailored advice to help you maximize savings and avoid pitfalls.

Section 3: Guidance on Choosing the Right Entity

Choosing the best business structure for your company is one of the most important decisions you'll make. It affects your taxes, legal protection, how you operate your business, and even your future growth potential. This isn't a decision to rush. Taking the time to weigh your options and understand what each structure offers can set you up for success. Below is an expanded guide to help you make the right choice:

1. Think About Your Goals

Start by defining both your short-term and long-term goals. Do you plan to keep your business small, like a local shop or home-based service? Or are you aiming to scale up quickly, attract investors, or even expand internationally? Your answer will guide your choice:

- **If simplicity matters most:** A Sole Proprietorship or Partnership might be ideal. These are easy to set up and maintain, which allows you to focus on your day-to-day operations.

- **If growth and investment are priorities:** Consider an LLC, S-Corp, or C-Corp. These structures are better equipped to handle complex needs like raising capital, adding partners, or issuing shares.

Also, think about how your industry and customer base align with your vision. For example, a tech startup with plans to raise venture capital would benefit from a C-Corp, while a freelance graphic designer might prefer a Sole Proprietorship for its simplicity.

2. Understand Your Risk

Different business structures offer different levels of personal liability protection. Ask yourself, "What's the worst-case scenario for my business?" If your business carries significant financial risks—like lawsuits, accidents, or large debts—you'll want a structure that protects your personal assets.

- **High-risk businesses:** If you're in industries like construction, manufacturing, or professional services, consider an LLC or Corporation. These separate your personal and business finances, limiting your personal liability.

- **Low-risk businesses:** Sole Proprietorships and Partnerships might suffice if you're running a small, low-risk operation. However, keep in mind that you're personally responsible for any business debts or lawsuits.

3. Learn About Taxes

Taxes can heavily influence your decision. Each structure has its own tax rules, and the right choice can save you significant money:

- **Sole Proprietorship and Partnerships:** These are "pass-through" entities, meaning business income is taxed on your personal return. While simple, this can result in higher taxes if your income grows.

- **LLC:** Offers flexibility. You can choose to be taxed as a Sole Proprietorship, Partnership, or Corporation depending on your situation.

- **S-Corp:** Helps you save on self-employment taxes by allowing you to pay yourself a salary and take distributions, which aren't subject to those taxes.

- **C-Corp:** Although it's subject to double taxation (corporate profits and shareholder dividends), it may be the best choice for large businesses or those reinvesting profits.

A tax expert can help you compare these options and decide which one minimizes your tax burden.

4. Think About Complexity

Some business structures are straightforward, while others come with more administrative work. Consider how much time and effort you can devote to managing legal and financial requirements:

- **Simple options:** Sole Proprietorships and Partnerships have minimal paperwork. They're ideal for new business owners who want to focus on growing their business rather than managing compliance.

- **More complex options:** LLCs and Corporations require formalities like annual reports, board meetings, and detailed tax filings. However, these added responsibilities come with benefits like liability protection and easier access to funding.

Make sure you're ready to handle the complexity before choosing a more formal structure.

5. Plan for the Future

Your business structure should support your long-term plans. If you anticipate bringing on investors, adding partners, or selling your business, some structures make these processes easier:

- **LLCs and Corporations:** These allow for flexible ownership and make it easier to transfer shares or bring in investors.

- **Sole Proprietorships and Partnerships:** These are less flexible. Transferring ownership or adding new partners can be complicated and may require restructuring the business.

Think about your exit strategy as well. If you plan to retire or sell your business, choosing the right structure now can save you headaches later.

6. Check State Laws

Every state has its own rules about business entities. Some states charge additional fees for LLCs or Corporations, while others offer tax advantages. For example, Delaware and Nevada are popular for their business-friendly laws, but they may not make sense for every business. Research your state's requirements or consult with a local expert to ensure compliance.

7. Get Professional Advice

While this guide provides a starting point, professional advice is invaluable. Here's who to consult:

- **Business Attorney:** They can explain legal risks, draft contracts, and help with liability protection.

- **Tax Expert:** They can show you how different structures affect your tax bill and help you choose the most cost-effective option.

- **Financial Advisor:** They can align your business structure with your overall financial goals, helping you plan for growth and stability.

8. Be Ready to Change

Your choice of business structure isn't permanent. As your business evolves, your needs may change. Many entrepreneurs start with a Sole Proprietorship or LLC because they're simple. Later, they switch to an S-Corp or C-Corp to handle growth, attract investors, or take advantage of tax savings.

Regularly review your structure to make sure it still fits your goals. Adjusting your structure as your business grows can help you avoid unnecessary costs or risks down the road.

By following these steps and seeking advice from professionals, you can choose a business structure that protects your interests and supports your vision. The right structure will make it easier to run your business, achieve your goals, and prepare for the future.

Chapter 11: Should I Pay Myself a Salary or Take Owner's Draws?

Section 1: Differences Between Salary and Owner's Draw

One of the biggest decisions small business owners face is figuring out the best way to pay themselves for their hard work. The two most common options are taking a salary or an owner's draw, and some people even use a mix of both. Each choice has different impacts on your taxes, cash flow, and legal responsibilities. By understanding these options and how they work, you can make the best choice for your business and personal finances.

What Is a Salary?

A salary is a set amount of money you pay yourself on a regular schedule, such as every two weeks or once a month. This is treated as wages, so taxes like federal and state income taxes, Social Security, and Medicare are automatically taken out. Salaries are managed through payroll systems to ensure everything is calculated and reported correctly.

If your business is set up as an S-Corporation or a C-Corporation and you work in the business, you are required to pay yourself a salary. The IRS expects this salary to be "reasonable" based on the type of work you do, your industry, and the size of your business. If the salary you set is too low, the IRS may impose penalties or question your tax filings.

One of the main advantages of taking a salary is the steady and predictable income it provides. This makes it easier to budget for personal expenses and save for future goals. However, taking a salary also involves extra responsibilities, like running payroll, keeping up with tax filings, and following employment regulations. While this might seem like a hassle, it's essential for staying compliant with tax laws and avoiding potential problems.

What Is an Owner's Draw?

An owner's draw is when you withdraw money from your business profits for personal use. Unlike a salary, this money isn't considered wages, so it doesn't go through payroll or have taxes taken out upfront. Instead, you'll pay taxes on it when you file your personal tax return. This includes self-employment taxes, which cover Social Security and Medicare.

Owner's draws are most common for sole proprietors, single-member LLCs, and partnerships. These types of businesses pass their profits directly to the owner's personal tax return, making it easy to take distributions as needed. One big advantage of owner's draws is flexibility. You can take money out of the business whenever you need it, and the amount can vary depending on how much your business earns.

However, this flexibility comes with some challenges. Without a regular schedule, it can be harder to plan your personal income and expenses. Taking out too much money can also hurt your business by leaving it without enough cash to cover operating costs or invest in growth opportunities. It's important to strike a balance between taking what you need and leaving enough for your business to thrive.

Key Differences

Aspect	Salary	Owner's Draw
Tax Withholding	Taxes withheld right away	Taxes paid later with personal return
Payroll Processing	Processed through payroll	No payroll needed
Legal Requirement	Required for S-Corps and C-Corps	Not required for sole proprietors, LLCs, or partnerships
Flexibility	Fixed and regular payments	Flexible timing and amount
IRS Scrutiny	Must be "reasonable"	Less scrutiny but must be reported correctly
Cash Flow Impact	Predictable expenses	Can be unpredictable

When to Use Each Option

- **Salary:** Salaries are best for business owners who work in S-Corporations or C-Corporations, where the IRS requires them. Salaries also provide a steady paycheck, which is helpful for personal budgeting and securing loans or mortgages. Lenders often prefer to see consistent income when evaluating loan applications.

- **Owner's Draw:** Draws are a good option for sole proprietors, partnerships, or LLCs that are taxed as pass-through entities. These businesses allow owners to take profits as needed, which is especially helpful if your income varies throughout the year or your business is still growing. Draws offer flexibility, but it's important to manage them carefully to avoid cash flow problems.

Additional Considerations

Sometimes, the best choice is to use both a salary and owner's draws. For example, if you own an S-Corporation, you might take a reasonable salary to meet IRS requirements and then use draws to supplement your income when your business earns more. This strategy can give you the predictability of a salary while still allowing some flexibility.

Understanding the differences between salaries and draws is key to making smart financial decisions. Choosing how to pay yourself affects not only your taxes but also your business's cash flow and long-term financial health. By carefully weighing your options, you can find the best balance for your business and personal needs. In the next sections, we'll explore tax rules and practical tips to help you get the most out of your pay.

Section 2: Tax Considerations

When deciding whether to pay yourself a salary or take owner's draws, it's important to understand how each option affects your taxes. This section breaks down how these methods work, what taxes you'll need to pay, and how they fit with different types of businesses. Choosing wisely can save money, ensure compliance, and help you plan better for your financial future.

1. Salary: Withholding and Payroll Taxes

If you pay yourself a salary, your business treats you like an employee. Here's what that means in greater detail:

- **Payroll Taxes:** Your business must withhold federal and state income taxes, Social Security, and Medicare taxes from your paycheck. Additionally, your business is responsible for paying an employer share of Social Security and Medicare taxes (FICA), which can add to its financial obligations. These contributions help fund your eventual benefits, like retirement Social Security payouts.

- **Unemployment Taxes:** In some states, even business owners need to pay state and federal unemployment taxes on their salaries. This requirement varies by location but can add to the complexity of compliance.

- **Paperwork:** Paying a salary comes with administrative responsibilities. Your salary must be reported on Form W-2, which is submitted annually to both you and the IRS. This documentation keeps everything above board and ensures you meet federal and state regulations.

Though handling payroll taxes and W-2 filings requires more effort, salaries simplify income tracking and enforce regularity. They also make it easier for you to budget for personal and household expenses, as you can rely on a steady income stream. Additionally, if your business operates as an S-Corp or C-Corp, paying yourself a reasonable salary is a legal expectation from the IRS.

2. Owner's Draw: Simpler but Requires Planning

An owner's draw lets you take money directly from the business profits without it being considered a formal paycheck. While simple on the surface, there are several tax implications to understand:

- **Self-Employment Taxes:** For sole proprietors, partners, or LLCs taxed as partnerships, your draws are not treated as wages. Instead, the income is part of your business's total earnings and is subject to self-employment taxes. These taxes include Social Security and Medicare and can account for over 15% of your net earnings.

- **No Automatic Tax Withholding:** Unlike with salaries, taxes are not automatically deducted from your draws. This means you're responsible for calculating and paying estimated quarterly taxes. Missing payments or underestimating can result in penalties.

- **Reporting:** Draws don't appear on a W-2 but are included in other parts of your tax return, like Schedule C for sole proprietors or Schedule K-1 for partnerships and S-Corps. This approach simplifies payroll management but shifts more responsibility to you for tracking income and tax obligations.

While draws offer flexibility and simplicity for many small businesses, they require discipline to ensure enough funds are set aside for taxes. Poor planning can lead to surprises at tax time and create cash flow issues.

3. IRS Rules: Reasonable Salary

If your business is an S-Corp or C-Corp and you actively work in the company, the IRS expects you to take a "reasonable salary" for the services you provide. This rule prevents business owners from avoiding payroll taxes by taking only draws. Here's what you need to know:

- **Avoiding Trouble:** If the IRS determines that your salary is unreasonably low, it may reclassify part of your draws as wages. This reclassification means paying back payroll taxes and could include interest and penalties.

- **What's Reasonable?:** The IRS looks at factors like your job duties, time spent working, and what people in similar roles are paid. Researching market rates or consulting a professional can help you determine the right amount. Keeping detailed records of how you calculate your salary can also protect you during an audit.

Paying yourself a reasonable salary can prevent complications and shows you're running your business responsibly.

4. Taxes by Business Type

Your type of business structure significantly impacts how you handle salaries and draws. Here's a breakdown:

- **Sole Proprietors and Partnerships:** These businesses do not allow for salaries. Owners take draws, and these are subject to self-employment taxes. The simplicity of this system makes it popular for small or one-person operations.

- **LLCs:** Single-member LLCs are taxed like sole proprietors, while multi-member LLCs are treated like partnerships. However, LLCs can elect to be taxed as S-Corps or C-Corps, which opens up the option of paying yourself a salary.

- **S-Corps:** If you own an S-Corp and work for the business, the IRS requires you to take a reasonable salary. Once that salary is established, any extra profits can be taken as draws, which aren't subject to self-employment taxes. This approach can reduce your overall tax burden if done correctly.

- **C-Corps:** With C-Corps, salaries are the primary way to pay yourself. You can also issue dividends, but these are taxed twice—first at the corporate level and then again when paid to you as an individual.

Understanding these distinctions ensures you pick a payment method that fits your business model and tax goals.

5. Planning and Paying Taxes

Regardless of whether you choose to pay yourself a salary, take draws, or use a mix of both, proper planning is essential:

- **Salaries:** With taxes automatically withheld, salaries reduce the risk of underpayment penalties and simplify compliance. They also provide a clear, predictable record of your income for both business and personal budgeting.

- **Draws:** When taking draws, you'll need to set aside funds for taxes and make quarterly payments. Good record-keeping and cash flow management are crucial to ensure you're prepared for these obligations.

Tax planning helps you avoid surprises and ensures smooth operations. Regular consultations with a tax professional can help you optimize your strategy, taking into account your business's financial health and your personal goals.

Conclusion

Salaries and draws both have their pros and cons. Your choice will depend on your business type, tax situation, and financial objectives. By understanding the tax implications, staying compliant with IRS rules, and planning ahead, you can minimize taxes, avoid penalties, and keep your business running smoothly. Consulting with experts when needed can ensure you're making the most informed decision possible.

Section 3: Best Practices for Paying Yourself

Paying yourself from your small business is more than just moving money into your personal bank account. It requires careful planning, smart decision-making, and ongoing attention. To do it right, you need to ensure that your pay fits your business's financial health and supports your goals. Below are some detailed tips to help you manage this effectively:

1. Decide on Fair Pay

Start by figuring out what a reasonable amount is for your role in the business. Here are a few factors to consider:

- **What Others Earn:** Research what people in similar roles and industries are earning. Use online tools, industry reports, and salary data to make comparisons. This will give you a clear idea of what is fair for your position.

- **How Your Business Is Doing:** Look closely at your income, expenses, and profit margins. Your pay should not hurt the business's ability to pay its bills, invest in growth, or maintain cash flow.

- **Your Effort and Skills:** Think about how much time you put into your business and the unique skills you bring. Your compensation should reflect the value of your contributions and the responsibilities you take on.

2. Plan Your Pay in the Budget

Include your salary or draws as part of your business budget to avoid overspending. Consider the following when planning:

- **Business Costs:** Make sure your regular expenses, such as rent, utilities, and supplies, are covered before setting your pay.
- **Taxes:** Allocate enough money to cover federal, state, and local taxes. This ensures you won't face surprises during tax season.
- **Savings for Growth:** Dedicate part of your profits to reinvest in the business. This might include buying new equipment, marketing, or hiring employees.

Having a clear budget ensures your business remains stable even during tough times.

3. Keep Personal and Business Money Separate

Mixing personal and business finances can create confusion and lead to problems. Here's how to keep them separate:

- **Separate Bank Accounts:** Use different accounts for business and personal transactions.

This makes tracking easier and ensures your books are accurate.

- **No Personal Expenses:** Avoid using your business funds for personal needs. If you need money, transfer it as a draw or salary.
- **Detailed Records:** Keep clear and complete records of all transactions to simplify tax filing and protect yourself in case of an audit.

This separation protects your business's financial health and keeps you organized.

4. Pay Yourself Consistently

Consistency is key when paying yourself. A predictable schedule helps you plan both your personal finances and your business cash flow. Here's how to stay consistent:

- **Salaries:** Set up a regular payroll system, paying yourself weekly or monthly. This ensures taxes are withheld correctly.
- **Draws:** If you're taking owner's draws, decide on a set schedule, like once a month or quarterly. Stick to this schedule to avoid cash flow surprises.

Consistent pay not only keeps your finances in order but also helps build good habits.

5. Follow Tax Rules

Paying taxes is non-negotiable, but the rules can vary based on how you pay yourself. Here's what to know:

- **Salaries:** If you take a salary, you need to withhold taxes like Social Security, Medicare, and income taxes. Make sure to file payroll tax forms on time.

- **Draws:** For owner's draws, save enough for self-employment taxes, which include Social Security and Medicare. Pay quarterly tax estimates to avoid penalties.

Using a tax professional or reliable software can help you stay compliant and avoid mistakes.

6. Check Your Pay Regularly

Your pay should adapt as your business grows or as circumstances change. Regularly review and adjust your compensation based on:

- **Revenue Changes:** If your business income increases or decreases, update your pay accordingly.

- **Market Rates:** Stay informed about what others in similar roles earn and adjust your compensation to stay competitive.

- **Personal Goals:** Align your pay with your financial goals, such as saving for retirement, a home, or other big purchases.

Frequent reviews keep your pay fair and in line with your needs and business goals.

7. Plan for the Future

As a business owner, it's your responsibility to plan for your future, including retirement and benefits. Here's what to think about:

- **Retirement Accounts:** Open a SEP IRA, Solo 401(k), or SIMPLE IRA to save for your future. These accounts often have tax advantages that can benefit both you and your business.

- **Health and Disability Insurance:** Budget for insurance to protect yourself and your family from unexpected medical expenses or income loss.

- **Additional Benefits:** Consider setting money aside for other benefits like vacation, professional development, or life insurance.

Planning ahead ensures you and your business are prepared for anything.

8. Write Down Your Plan

Documentation is essential to protect yourself and your business. Make sure to:

- Keep notes about how you calculate your salary or draws.

- Save copies of financial statements that support your decisions.

- Maintain accurate tax and payroll records.

Having a written record makes it easier to answer questions or resolve disputes if they arise.

9. Ask for Help

Getting advice from experts can make paying yourself simpler and more effective. Here's how they can help:

- **Tax Professionals:** They can help you minimize taxes and ensure compliance.
- **Financial Advisors:** They can help you balance personal pay with business growth and savings goals.
- **Business Coaches:** They can provide insights on managing finances and scaling your business.

Consulting with these experts can save you time, money, and stress.

By following these detailed tips, you can pay yourself in a way that rewards your effort while keeping your business on the path to success. Planning, consistency, and smart decisions make all the difference.

Chapter 12: What Expenses Are Tax-Deductible for My Small Business?

Section 1: Common Deductible Expenses

Understanding which expenses are tax-deductible is essential for small business owners looking to reduce their taxable income legally. The IRS allows deductions for ordinary and necessary business expenses, which are costs common in your industry and helpful for running your business. Below is an expanded list of common deductible expenses, along with detailed explanations and tips to help you maximize your tax savings.

1. **Office Supplies** Everyday items like paper, pens, printer ink, and staplers are deductible if they are used exclusively for your business. This category also includes more specialized supplies such as binders, storage solutions, and technical tools needed for specific industries, such as drafting equipment for architects or cooking utensils for chefs. Additionally, any software or small tools used for daily operations, like accounting software or scheduling apps, can be deducted. Subscriptions to business-related services, such as cloud storage, office productivity software, or even industry-specific tools like graphic design programs, fall under this category. It's important to note that even small purchases, like USB drives or replacement cords, should be tracked and recorded. Always keep receipts and documentation to substantiate these purchases,

as this will be crucial in the event of an audit. Maintaining organized records, such as using a digital receipt tracker, can simplify this process and help you claim all eligible deductions without hassle.

2. **Rent and Utilities** If you lease office space, the cost of rent is fully deductible. This includes not only monthly rent payments but also any associated costs such as maintenance fees, parking fees tied to the office lease, or property management fees if these are part of your rental agreement. Utilities, including electricity, water, internet, and heating for your business premises, are also deductible. For example, if you subscribe to a business-grade internet service, the full cost is deductible. For home-based businesses, you may be able to claim a portion of these expenses through the home office deduction, provided the space is used regularly and exclusively for business purposes. This can include a proportional share of rent or mortgage interest, property taxes, and homeowners' insurance premiums. This deduction requires detailed records, such as utility bills and floor plans showing the percentage of your home used for work. Many business owners find it helpful to use expense tracking apps or dedicated spreadsheets to log and calculate these shared costs. Additionally, if your business operates out of a co-working space, the membership or rental fees for that space are also deductible. These

expanded guidelines ensure you can account for all eligible costs and maximize your deductions.

3. **Employee Wages and Benefits** Salaries, wages, bonuses, and commissions paid to employees are deductible. This includes not only regular payroll but also incentive-based compensation such as performance bonuses or sales commissions. Additionally, employer-provided benefits, such as health insurance, life insurance, and retirement plan contributions, can also be deducted. These benefits may extend to programs like employee wellness initiatives, gym memberships, or tuition reimbursement plans if they are part of the company's benefits policy. Costs associated with hiring independent contractors or freelancers are equally deductible, provided you issue the necessary tax forms (e.g., 1099-NEC) and maintain detailed records of payments and service agreements. If you offer professional development opportunities to your staff, such as training programs or certifications, those expenses are also deductible. Remember to include payroll taxes you pay as an employer, including Social Security and Medicare contributions, as part of your deductible expenses. Maintaining comprehensive payroll records will help ensure you claim all eligible deductions while staying compliant with tax regulations.

4. **Professional Services** Fees paid to lawyers, accountants, consultants, and other professionals

for business-related services are deductible. This includes services like legal advice for contracts, intellectual property filings, or dispute resolution, and accounting help for financial planning or tax preparation. Hiring a tax preparer to file your business taxes or a lawyer to draft contracts would qualify. Additionally, fees for consultants who provide expertise in marketing, IT systems, or business strategy are also covered. If you use managed services for payroll, bookkeeping, or financial reporting, subscription costs for the software or platforms they use can also be deducted. This extends to retainer fees for ongoing professional support, making it crucial to document all agreements and invoices. Keeping a detailed log of these professional expenses ensures you maximize deductions while staying organized for tax season.

5. **Marketing and Advertising** Costs associated with promoting your business, including digital ads, social media campaigns, printed materials, and website design, are deductible. This category also includes expenses for email marketing platforms, subscription fees for analytics tools, and costs for content creation like photography or videography services for promotional purposes. Sponsorships for community events or partnerships with influencers to boost brand visibility are also deductible. Branded merchandise, such as custom apparel, mugs, or tote bags designed to promote your company,

qualifies as well. Fees for search engine optimization (SEO) services, including keyword research and website enhancements, fall into this category, alongside payments to advertising agencies or freelancers who manage your campaigns. Small businesses often overlook deductions for social media management tools, scheduling apps, and even paid boosts for social posts, all of which are eligible. Additionally, if you purchase ad space in traditional media like newspapers, magazines, or radio, these costs are fully deductible. Keeping an organized record of all invoices, contracts, and receipts related to marketing efforts ensures you maximize these deductions.

6. **Business Travel** Expenses for travel related to your business, such as airfare, hotel accommodations, and rental cars, are deductible. This includes incidental expenses like baggage fees, tips for hotel staff, or Wi-Fi costs during your trip. If you incur costs for public transportation, such as subways, buses, or taxis, these are also deductible. Meals during business travel are partially deductible, typically at 50% of the cost, though under certain IRS guidelines, the deduction rate may temporarily increase. Be sure to document the purpose of the trip and keep itemized receipts to support these claims. Additionally, travel-related fees, such as passport renewals or expedited visa services directly tied to business activities, may also qualify. If you use

a personal vehicle for business travel, tracking mileage or fuel expenses is essential. Consider using an app or a detailed logbook to record dates, destinations, and miles driven, as the IRS requires precise documentation to substantiate these deductions. Furthermore, if the travel involves attending conferences, trade shows, or client meetings, associated costs like registration fees and shipping promotional materials are also deductible. By carefully planning and recording these expenses, you can maximize your tax savings while ensuring compliance with tax regulations.

7. **Vehicle Expenses** If you use a vehicle for business purposes, you can deduct either the actual expenses (e.g., gas, maintenance, insurance, registration fees, and repairs) or use the standard mileage rate set by the IRS. Actual expenses can also include depreciation for owned vehicles or lease payments for leased vehicles, prorated for business use. To determine which method provides the greater deduction, you can calculate both and choose the more favorable option. Make sure to track business mileage meticulously, using a logbook or a mileage-tracking app, and record the purpose of each trip, the starting and ending locations, and the total distance traveled. Note that commuting expenses to and from a regular place of business are not deductible. However, travel between multiple work locations or for client meetings is

fully deductible. Additionally, parking fees and tolls incurred during business trips can be added to the deductible amount, whether using the actual expense method or the standard mileage rate. Maintaining comprehensive records ensures compliance and maximizes your deduction potential.

8. **Insurance** Business insurance premiums, such as general liability insurance, professional liability insurance, and property insurance, are deductible. This deduction can extend to specialized coverage tailored to your industry, such as cyber liability insurance for businesses handling sensitive data or product liability insurance for manufacturers. Health insurance premiums for self-employed individuals may also qualify, provided they meet IRS requirements. Workers' compensation insurance and unemployment insurance paid for employees are fully deductible, helping businesses cover the risks associated with their workforce. If you're running a home-based business, consider including renters' or homeowners' insurance for the portion of your home used exclusively for work. This allocation must be calculated based on the square footage or percentage of your home dedicated to business activities. Additionally, umbrella insurance policies that provide overarching coverage for business risks may also qualify if they relate directly to your operations. Keeping detailed records of policy

payments, coverage details, and correspondence with insurers ensures accurate reporting and maximized deductions.

9. **Education and Training** Costs for attending workshops, courses, and conferences that improve your skills or knowledge for your business are deductible. This includes online training and certification programs directly related to your business activities, such as learning new software relevant to your industry or gaining additional qualifications to enhance your services. Membership fees for professional organizations, which often provide networking opportunities, industry-specific resources, and discounted training programs, can also qualify as deductions. Subscriptions to industry publications, whether in print or digital formats, are another eligible expense, offering valuable insights and keeping you updated on trends and best practices in your field. If you host or sponsor educational events, like webinars or in-house training for your team, the associated costs—including materials, speaker fees, and venue rental—may also be deductible. Additionally, certifications required to maintain professional licenses or credentials, such as continuing education courses for accountants or real estate agents, are considered legitimate deductions. Keep detailed records, including receipts, invoices, and course descriptions, to substantiate

these claims and maximize the potential tax benefits of investing in education and training.

10. **Depreciation** You can deduct the depreciation of business assets, such as computers, machinery, and office furniture, over time. This allows businesses to recover the cost of significant purchases by spreading the deduction across the useful life of the asset as determined by the IRS. Assets like vehicles, equipment, and even improvements to leased properties often qualify for depreciation. In some cases, businesses can take advantage of accelerated depreciation methods, such as Section 179 expensing, which permits the immediate deduction of certain asset purchases up to an annual limit. Bonus depreciation may also apply, allowing businesses to write off a large percentage of asset costs in the first year. To ensure compliance, maintain detailed records of each asset, including purchase price, date of acquisition, and documentation supporting its business use. Depreciation schedules can be complex, so consulting a tax professional or using specialized accounting software is recommended to maximize your deductions and adhere to IRS requirements.

11. **Loan Interest and Bank Fees** Interest on business loans and fees for maintaining business bank accounts or credit cards are deductible. This includes interest on loans taken to purchase equipment, expand operations, or meet

operational needs, as well as fees for loan origination or early repayment penalties. Bank account maintenance fees, wire transfer charges, and even charges for overdraft protection linked to your business account can also be deducted. However, personal loan interest is not deductible, even if the funds are used for business purposes. To ensure clarity and compliance, always separate your business and personal finances by using dedicated business bank accounts and credit cards. This not only simplifies the tracking of deductible expenses but also avoids complications during tax filing. Maintain records of all interest payments, loan agreements, and bank statements to substantiate your claims in case of an audit.

12. **Taxes and Licenses** State and local taxes related to your business, such as business license fees, property taxes, and payroll taxes, are deductible. Self-employment taxes are partially deductible as well, specifically the employer-equivalent portion. If you're required to collect sales tax, note that this isn't deductible, but the cost of compliance tools or services can be.

13. **Miscellaneous Operating Costs** Many small business owners overlook deductions for miscellaneous operating costs, such as telephone expenses, internet costs, or shipping fees. Expenses for tools, equipment, or furniture under a certain threshold may also qualify for immediate expensing rather than depreciation.

By understanding and properly categorizing these common deductible expenses, you can ensure you're taking full advantage of tax benefits while maintaining compliance with IRS regulations. The key is to maintain clear, accurate records, utilize software tools where possible, and consult a tax professional if you have questions about specific deductions. Proper planning and documentation can significantly impact your bottom line and keep your financial operations running smoothly.

Section 2: Lesser-Known Deductions to Consider

While many small business owners are familiar with common tax deductions like office supplies, travel expenses, and advertising costs, there are several lesser-known deductions that can significantly reduce your taxable income. By exploring these opportunities, you can ensure you're maximizing your savings while staying compliant with tax regulations. Here are some deductions you may not have considered:

1. Startup Costs

If your business is in its first year of operation, you can deduct up to $5,000 in startup costs, which can include expenses for market research, legal fees, and employee training. Additionally, costs such as licensing fees, permits, and equipment setup can qualify. Any expenses exceeding this limit can be amortized over 15 years, ensuring you can spread out the benefits.

2. Educational Expenses

The cost of courses, workshops, certifications, and even relevant books or online subscriptions that help you improve your skills or expand your expertise in your field can be deducted as long as they are directly related to your business. However, there are limitations to keep in mind. These expenses must directly benefit your current business operations and cannot qualify if they prepare you for a new line of work. For example, a marketing professional can deduct a social media advertising workshop but not a course in culinary arts unless it aligns with their existing business. Additionally, the IRS requires proper documentation, such as receipts, detailed course descriptions, and proof of payment, to validate these claims. This includes costs for webinars, industry conferences, and software tutorials, enabling continuous learning that benefits your operations within the scope of your current business activities.

3. Health Insurance Premiums

If you're self-employed and not eligible for health coverage through a spouse's plan, you can deduct the premiums you pay for health, dental, and long-term care insurance for yourself, your spouse, and your dependents. This deduction can significantly lower your taxable income while addressing essential personal needs. However, it is important to note that this deduction is limited to your net profit from self-employment. If your business operates at a loss, you won't be able to claim this deduction. Additionally, the deduction does not apply to any portion of the premiums that are paid for coverage under a subsidized plan available through your spouse's employer. To claim this deduction, you must ensure the premiums are not already being covered by a tax-advantaged account such as an HSA or FSA, and you should maintain proper documentation, such as proof of payments and policy details, to support your claim in case of an audit.

4. Bad Debts

If your business extends credit to customers and you are unable to collect payment, you may be able to write off these bad debts. This deduction is typically applicable to businesses that use accrual accounting. Examples include unpaid invoices, dishonored checks, and loans made to customers or vendors.

5. Home Office Deduction

For business owners who operate out of their homes, the home office deduction allows you to deduct a portion of your rent or mortgage, utilities, and maintenance expenses. To qualify, the space must be used exclusively and regularly for business purposes. This means the area must be a distinct part of your home, such as a room or clearly defined space, and cannot serve dual purposes, like being used as both an office and a guest bedroom.

The IRS offers two methods for claiming this deduction:

1. **Actual Expense Method:** Under this method, you calculate the actual expenses incurred for the business use of your home. This includes a

portion of your mortgage interest, property taxes, utilities, insurance, depreciation, and maintenance costs, based on the percentage of your home's square footage used for business.

2. **Simplified Method:** This option allows you to claim $5 per square foot of your home office, up to a maximum of 300 square feet, resulting in a maximum deduction of $1,500. While simpler to calculate, this method may result in a smaller deduction compared to the actual expense method.

It's important to note that the home office deduction is available to self-employed individuals and certain employees, but not to employees who work from home unless they meet stringent IRS requirements. Accurate record-keeping, such as utility bills, receipts for repairs, and a floor plan with measurements of the office space, is essential to substantiate your claim. Failure to meet these criteria can result in the disallowance of the deduction.

6. Bank Fees and Interest

Fees for maintaining a business bank account or merchant account, as well as interest paid on business loans or credit cards, can be deducted as business expenses. This includes charges for overdrafts, wire transfers, and annual credit card fees, provided these accounts are exclusively used for your business.

7. Business Use of Your Vehicle

If you use your personal vehicle for business purposes, you can deduct the mileage or actual expenses like gas, maintenance, insurance, and depreciation. There are two methods for claiming this deduction:

1. **Standard Mileage Rate:** You can deduct a set amount per mile driven for business purposes. The IRS updates this rate annually; for example, in recent years, it has ranged between 56 and 65 cents per mile. To use this method, you must track all business-related mileage throughout the year using a logbook or mileage-tracking app.

2. **Actual Expense Method:** With this method, you can deduct the actual costs of operating your vehicle for business, including gas, maintenance, insurance, lease payments, depreciation, and repairs. However, you must calculate the percentage of vehicle use dedicated to business purposes versus personal use and apply this percentage to the total expenses.

Limitations and Considerations

- **Commuting Costs:** Travel between your home and your regular place of business is considered commuting and is not deductible. However, travel between multiple business locations or for client visits is deductible.

- **Documentation Requirements:** Regardless of the method chosen, the IRS requires detailed records, including dates, purposes, destinations, and odometer readings, to validate your claims.

- **Exclusivity for Business Use:** If you use the vehicle for both personal and business purposes, you cannot claim 100% of expenses. Accurately calculating and documenting the business-use percentage is crucial.

By understanding these methods and limitations, you can choose the deduction approach that provides the greatest tax benefit while maintaining compliance with IRS regulations.

8. Retirement Plan Contributions

Contributions to retirement plans like SEP IRAs, SIMPLE IRAs, or solo 401(k)s are deductible and can help reduce your taxable income while planning for your future. Here is a detailed breakdown of each plan, along with their advantages and limitations:

1. **SEP IRA (Simplified Employee Pension Individual Retirement Account):**
    - **Advantages:**
        - Easy to set up and maintain, making it suitable for small businesses and self-employed individuals.
        - High contribution limits (up to 25% of compensation or $66,000 in 2023, whichever is less).

- Employer-only contributions, which provide flexibility in deciding how much to contribute each year.
  - **Limitations:**
    - Contributions must be made for all eligible employees, including part-time workers who meet certain criteria.
    - Employees cannot contribute to the plan directly.

2. **SIMPLE IRA (Savings Incentive Match Plan for Employees):**
   - **Advantages:**
     - Employers can either match employee contributions up to 3% of their salary or make a fixed 2% contribution regardless of employee participation.
     - Employee contributions are allowed, with limits of up to $15,500 in 2023 (or $19,000 for those aged 50 or older).
     - Easier administration compared to traditional 401(k) plans.

- **Limitations:**
  - Lower contribution limits compared to other plans like SEP IRAs or solo 401(k)s.
  - Mandatory employer contributions can be a financial commitment.

3. **Solo 401(k):**
   - **Advantages:**
     - Ideal for self-employed individuals or business owners with no employees (except a spouse).
     - Higher contribution limits due to the ability to contribute both as an employer and an employee. For 2023, the employee contribution limit is $22,500 (or $30,000 if aged 50 or older), plus up to 25% of business profits as the employer.
     - Option to include a Roth component for after-tax contributions, allowing for tax-free withdrawals in retirement.
   - **Limitations:**
     - More complex setup and administration compared to SEP or SIMPLE IRAs.

- Strict eligibility requirements; adding employees disqualifies you from using this plan.

Each plan has its own rules and benefits, so it's essential to consider your business structure, financial goals, and administrative capacity when selecting one. Consulting with a financial advisor or tax professional can help you choose the most advantageous plan for your situation.

9. Phone and Internet Costs

If you use your phone or internet for business purposes, you can deduct a portion of these expenses. Make sure to calculate the percentage based on your business versus personal use. Costs for business-related apps, subscriptions, and software tied to phone or internet services are also deductible.

10. Professional Memberships and Subscriptions

Fees for industry-specific memberships, professional organizations, and trade journals that are directly related to your business are deductible. These expenses support networking and knowledge acquisition, which are integral to your professional growth.

11. Marketing and Promotional Gifts

If you give gifts to clients or business associates, you can deduct up to $25 per person annually. While the deduction is limited, branded items, customized merchandise, or high-value cards can enhance your client relationships while remaining within the deductible limits.

12. Tax Preparation and Consulting Fees

The cost of hiring a tax professional or consultant for your business is deductible, as are the fees for accounting software and tax preparation tools. This includes ongoing bookkeeping services or software subscriptions designed to manage your finances.

13. Energy-Efficient Improvements

If you own a commercial property and make energy-efficient upgrades like installing solar panels, energy-efficient HVAC systems, or insulation improvements, you may qualify for specific tax credits and deductions. With the passage of the Inflation Reduction Act (IRA), these credits have been expanded and extended, making them even more beneficial for business owners. For instance, the Investment Tax Credit (ITC) for solar energy systems now offers a 30% federal tax credit on the total installation costs, with additional bonuses for projects meeting certain labor and domestic content requirements.

Additionally, deductions under Section 179D for energy-efficient commercial buildings have been enhanced. The IRA increases the deduction amount based on energy savings achieved and ensures that even smaller projects can qualify. For state-level incentives, these often complement federal credits, offering rebates or additional tax benefits that vary by location. To take full advantage of these programs, it's critical to consult with an energy auditor or tax professional who can guide you through the qualifying criteria and documentation requirements. Keep in mind that these credits and deductions often require certifications or compliance with specific energy standards, so planning upgrades with these conditions in mind is essential.

14. Travel for Business Purposes

Travel expenses, including airfare, lodging, meals, and transportation for business trips, are deductible. However, the rules surrounding these deductions have evolved, and it is essential to understand the nuances:

1. **Airfare and Transportation:** Costs for flights, taxis, rental cars, and ride-sharing services are deductible if the primary purpose of the trip is business-related. Personal travel expenses, such as sightseeing or recreational activities, are not deductible.

2. **Lodging:** Hotel stays are deductible for the days you are conducting business. If you extend your trip for personal reasons, only the lodging costs incurred during the business portion are deductible.

3. **Meals:** Business-related meals during travel are 50% deductible. This includes meals with clients or during conferences. Ensure you keep itemized receipts and document the purpose of the meal and the attendees. Under temporary pandemic-related relief, certain meal deductions (e.g., those provided by restaurants) may qualify for 100% deduction for specific tax years.

4. **Conferences and Networking Events:** Costs associated with attending conferences, trade

shows, or industry networking events are deductible if directly related to your business.

Key Limitations and Documentation Requirements

- **Dual Purpose Trips:** If a trip combines business and personal activities, you can only deduct expenses directly related to the business portion. For example, airfare to a business meeting is deductible, but expenses for a vacation added to the trip are not.

- **Strict Documentation:** The IRS requires detailed records, including receipts, itineraries, and notes explaining the business purpose of the trip. For meals, include the names of attendees and the topics discussed.

- **Non-Deductible Costs:** Personal expenses, such as entertainment, fines, or luxury upgrades, are not deductible under any circumstances.

By understanding these updated rules and maintaining meticulous records, you can ensure compliance while maximizing your allowable deductions for business travel.

Tips for Maximizing Lesser-Known Deductions

- **Stay Organized:** Keep detailed and categorized records of all your expenses throughout the year. Maintain a digital or physical filing system for receipts and invoices.

- **Consult a Professional:** A tax professional can help identify deductions that apply to your unique business circumstances. They can also advise you on documentation requirements to avoid penalties or disallowed deductions.

- **Use Technology:** Accounting software can simplify tracking and categorizing expenses, making it easier to claim deductions accurately. Some tools offer features like automatic categorization, receipt scanning, and integration with your bank accounts.

- **Review Annually:** Tax laws change frequently. Review your eligible deductions annually to ensure compliance and take advantage of new opportunities.

By being aware of these lesser-known deductions and maintaining meticulous records, you can reduce your tax liability and keep more of your hard-earned money in your business. Proactively seeking out opportunities to save can make a significant difference in your financial health over time.

Section 3: Keeping Records for Deductions

Keeping good records is important for making sure you can claim tax deductions and follow IRS rules. Proper documentation protects your business during an audit and helps you get the most out of your deductions. A simple system makes tax prep easier, highlights savings, and avoids penalties. Here are some key tips for keeping track of deductible expenses:

1. Know What the IRS Needs

The IRS says business expenses must be ordinary and necessary to count as deductions. Ordinary expenses are common in your line of work, and necessary expenses are helpful for running your business. Your records should show the amount, date, and purpose of each expense. Examples of proof include:

- Receipts
- Invoices
- Bank and credit card statements
- Canceled checks
- Contracts or agreements

Some deductions, like car expenses or travel costs, may need extra proof. For example, keep a mileage log for vehicle use and travel plans that show the business reason and who was involved. Being thorough ensures you can back up your claims in case of an audit.

2. Use Digital Tools

Digital tools make it easier to stay organized and avoid losing important records. Try these options:

- **Bookkeeping Software**: Programs like QuickBooks, Xero, or Wave can automatically track and sort your expenses. Many link to your bank for easy updates.

- **Receipt Apps**: Use apps like Expensify or Shoeboxed to scan and store receipts. Many bookkeeping programs also include receipt storage.

- **Cloud Storage**: Save copies of receipts, invoices, and other documents in a cloud service like Google Drive or Dropbox. This keeps them safe and easy to find.
- **Automation Tools**: Automating tasks like sorting expenses or making reports saves time and reduces mistakes.

3. Sort Records by Category

Sorting records by expense categories makes tax time easier and helps you avoid missing anything. It also gives you a better idea of where your money is going. Common categories include:

- Office supplies
- Advertising and marketing
- Travel and meals
- Professional services (e.g., lawyers, accountants)
- Rent or lease payments
- Utilities
- Technology (e.g., software, subscriptions, equipment)

Create folders or use tags for each category. Update your records regularly so everything is ready when you need it. You can also make subcategories for more detailed tracking.

4. Log Vehicle Use

If you use your car for business, you can deduct mileage or actual expenses. To meet IRS rules, keep a log with:

- The date of the trip
- Starting and ending locations
- Why the trip was for business
- Starting and ending mileage

Apps like MileIQ or Everlance can track your mileage automatically. Also, save receipts for parking, tolls, or car maintenance related to business use, as these are easy to forget.

5. Home Office Records

If you claim a home office deduction, keep detailed records like:

- The size of your office compared to your home's total area
- Bills for utilities and maintenance
- Lease agreements or mortgage statements
- Photos of your workspace to show it's only for business
- Internet and phone bills, with the business-use percentage calculated

The IRS also offers a simplified home office deduction method, which reduces paperwork but might not give as large a deduction.

6. Track Meals and Entertainment Carefully

Meals and entertainment have special rules. For meals, keep:

- Receipts showing the cost
- Why the meal was for business
- Names of people or organizations involved

Usually, only 50% of meal costs can be deducted. Entertainment expenses aren't usually deductible, but there are exceptions for business events. Using a log or app can help you keep track of these expenses properly.

7. Know How Long to Keep Records

The IRS says to keep tax records for three years after filing your return. In some cases, you need to keep them longer:

- **Six years**: If you underreport income by more than 25%.
- **Seven years**: If you claim a loss from worthless investments or bad debts.
- **Indefinitely**: If you don't file a return or file a fraudulent one.

Even for non-deductible expenses, keeping records for three years can be helpful during an audit.

8. Work with a Tax Professional

A tax expert can help you figure out what records you need and make sure they meet IRS standards. They can also recommend tools and strategies for your type of business and alert you to deductions you might miss. A good relationship with a tax advisor helps you stay prepared for changes in tax laws.

Summary

Keeping good records is the key to claiming the right tax deductions. By understanding IRS rules, using helpful tools, and organizing your documents, you'll be ready for tax season and avoid risks during an audit. Setting up a solid system for record-keeping saves time, money, and stress, helping your business grow while staying compliant.

Chapter 13: How Do I Claim the QBID (Qualified Business Income Deduction)?

Section 1: Overview of the QBID

The Qualified Business Income Deduction (QBID) is a major tax benefit for small business owners. It was introduced in 2017 as part of the Tax Cuts and Jobs Act (TCJA). This deduction lets qualified taxpayers lower their taxable income by up to 20% of their qualified business income (QBI). By reducing the amount of income that gets taxed, the QBID can save business owners a lot of money, making it an important tool for managing taxes.

What is Qualified Business Income? Qualified Business Income, or QBI, is the money you earn from running a qualified business. This includes income from businesses like sole proprietorships, partnerships, S corporations, and some LLCs. QBI includes the income, gains, deductions, and losses related to the business. However, not all types of income count as QBI. For example, capital gains, dividend income, and interest from investments are not included. Also, wages you pay yourself as a W-2 employee from your business do not count as QBI. This means the deduction focuses on the profits of the business, not the salary you earn.

Who Can Claim the QBID? The QBID is available to individuals, trusts, and estates that report QBI from a U.S.-based trade or business. This deduction applies to pass-through businesses, where the business income is included on the owner's personal tax return. Examples of pass-through businesses are sole proprietorships, partnerships, and S corporations. On the other hand, C corporations cannot claim this deduction because their income is taxed at the corporate level.

Key Features of the QBID

1. **20% Deduction:** Eligible taxpayers can deduct up to 20% of their QBI. However, there are rules and limits, especially for people with high incomes.

2. **Thresholds and Phase-Outs:** The QBID's value depends on how much taxable income you have. If your income is above a certain level, the deduction might be reduced or unavailable. This is especially true for certain jobs like law, accounting, consulting, or healthcare, which face stricter rules if income exceeds the limits.

3. **W-2 Wages and Property Factor:** For people with high incomes, the deduction may depend on the amount of wages paid to employees and the value of business property. These rules encourage businesses to hire workers and invest in assets.

4. **Complex Rules:** The QBID has many rules that depend on your income, the type of business you run, and how you file your taxes. Sometimes, figuring out how to qualify for the deduction can require help from a tax expert.

Why is the QBID Important? The QBID doesn't just save you money on taxes right now—it can help your business in the long run. By lowering the taxes on your business profits, it gives you more cash to work with. This extra money can be used to hire employees, buy new equipment, or expand your business. It also gives you a safety net for unexpected expenses or opportunities.

Understanding the QBID is key to smart tax planning. Knowing how to qualify for the deduction and get the most from it can be a big help for your overall financial goals. For example, some business owners might adjust their business structure or income to make sure they qualify for the full deduction.

In short, the QBID is a valuable tool for reducing taxes and keeping more of your business earnings. It helps small business owners improve their financial stability and invest in future growth, making it an essential part of effective tax management.

Section 2: Eligibility Requirements for the QBID

To use this deduction, you need to meet specific rules. This section explains them in simple terms.

1. What Kinds of Businesses Qualify?

The QBID is meant for "pass-through" businesses, which means the business income is taxed on the owner's personal tax return instead of at the business level. The types of businesses that qualify are:

- **Sole Proprietorships**: Businesses owned and run by one person.
- **Partnerships**: Businesses owned by two or more people who share the profits.
- **S Corporations**: Small corporations where the profits are passed to the shareholders.
- **LLCs**: Limited liability companies taxed like one of the above.

C corporations do not qualify because their profits are taxed separately from the owners.

2. What Counts as Qualified Business Income (QBI)?

QBI is the profit your business earns after subtracting expenses. However, not all income qualifies. Here's what counts and what doesn't:

Included in QBI:

- Business profits after expenses and deductions.

Not Included in QBI:

- Capital gains or losses (from selling property or investments).
- Dividends (money earned from stocks).
- Interest income (unless it's directly tied to your business).

- Wages or guaranteed payments you receive from your business.

It's important to separate QBI from other types of income when calculating the deduction.

3. How Much Can You Earn and Still Qualify?

The amount you can deduct depends on your total taxable income (before the QBID is applied). For the 2024 tax year:

- **Single Filers**: If you earn $182,100 or less, you qualify for the full QBID.
- **Married Filing Jointly**: If you earn $364,200 or less, you qualify for the full QBID.

If your income is above these amounts, you may still qualify, but there are extra rules that apply (explained below).

4. What if Your Business Is in Certain Fields (SSTB Rules)?

Some businesses are considered **Specified Service Trades or Businesses (SSTBs)**. These are businesses where the main value comes from the owner's or employees' skills or reputation. Examples of SSTBs include:

- Health care professionals (like doctors and dentists).

- Legal professionals (like lawyers).
- Accountants and financial advisors.
- Consultants.
- Artists and performers (like actors and musicians).

If your business is an SSTB:

- You qualify for the QBID if your taxable income is **below** the threshold.
- If your taxable income is **above** the threshold, the deduction gets smaller and disappears completely at a certain point (around $232,100 for single filers and $464,200 for married filing jointly).

5. How Do Wages and Investments Affect the Deduction?

For people earning more than the income limit, the QBID is capped. The deduction will be the lesser of:

1. **20% of QBI**, or
2. **The greater of**:
    - 50% of wages the business paid to employees, or
    - 25% of wages the business paid, **plus** 2.5% of the value of the business's property (like equipment or buildings).

Example: If your business owns expensive equipment or buildings, you might still qualify for the deduction even if you don't pay much in wages.

6. How Does This Work for Partnerships and S Corporations?

For partnerships and S corporations, the QBID is calculated at the **owner's level**, not the business's. The business gives each owner or shareholder a Schedule K-1 form that shows their share of the income and other details. Each owner then figures out their own QBID based on their personal taxes.

7. Does the Business Need to Be in the U.S.?

Yes. The QBID only applies to income earned from business operations in the United States. If your business earns money from foreign activities or investments, that income does not qualify for the deduction.

8. Who Can Claim the QBID?

The deduction is available to individuals, trusts, and estates. Corporations cannot claim the QBID, since it's specifically for pass-through income.

By knowing these rules, you can figure out if you qualify for the QBID. If your income is higher than the threshold or your business falls under the SSTB category, you might need to plan ahead to get the most out of this deduction. In the next section, we'll share tips on how to maximize the QBID and lower your tax bill.

Section 3: Tips for Maximizing the QBID

The QBID is a powerful way to lower your taxes, but to get the most out of it, you need to plan carefully and understand the rules. By managing your business finances wisely and staying informed, you can maximize this valuable tax benefit. Here are detailed tips to help you make the most of the QBID:

1. Keep Clear Records of Income and Expenses

Good bookkeeping is essential to ensure you include all eligible income and expenses. This not only helps you calculate your Qualified Business Income (QBI) but also prevents mistakes that could reduce your deduction or lead to IRS issues.

- Use reliable tools like QuickBooks, Xero, or Wave to track your income and expenses.
- Regularly review your bank and credit card statements to make sure your financial records are accurate and up-to-date.
- Separate personal and business expenses to avoid confusion, errors, and potential penalties.
- Keep organized records of receipts, invoices, and other financial documents, either digitally or in

physical files, to substantiate your deductions if needed.

- Schedule regular check-ins to review your books and address any discrepancies promptly.

2. Understand Income Limits

The QBID comes with income limits, which means your deduction could be reduced or eliminated if you earn too much. Understanding these limits can help you plan and stay eligible for the full deduction.

- Monitor your taxable income throughout the year, especially if you expect major changes in your income.

- If you're close to the limit, consider deferring some income to the next year or accelerating deductible expenses into the current year.

- Contribute to tax-advantaged accounts like 401(k)s, IRAs, or HSAs to lower your taxable income while saving for retirement or healthcare expenses.

- Review additional sources of income that might push you over the limit and strategize ways to manage them effectively.

- Use tax planning software or consult a professional to model your income and deductions in different scenarios.

3. Maximize W-2 Wages and Property

If your business employs workers or owns property, these factors can directly affect your QBID. Ensuring you have enough wages or property can help you maximize your deduction.

- Evaluate your payroll setup and make necessary adjustments to meet QBID rules, such as paying reasonable wages to yourself or your employees.

- Ensure that the value of any property your business owns is properly calculated and reported to qualify for the deduction.

- Consider purchasing or upgrading equipment, real estate, or other assets that qualify as business property under QBID rules.

- Time significant purchases or investments in property to align with your QBID strategy and maximize the deduction.

- Review depreciation schedules for assets to ensure they are appropriately included in your calculations.

4. Pick the Best Business Structure

Your business's structure can influence how your QBID is calculated. Certain structures, like S-Corporations or partnerships, may offer more advantages than others.

- Assess your current business structure and consult with a tax professional to determine if restructuring could increase your QBID.

- Weigh the benefits of restructuring, such as increased deductions, against the potential costs, including administrative and legal fees.

- Understand how each type of business entity impacts your tax liability, reporting requirements, and eligibility for QBID benefits.

- For sole proprietors, consider if incorporating or forming an LLC would provide additional QBID benefits while protecting your personal assets.

5. Use Aggregation Rules

The IRS allows you to combine related businesses for QBID purposes, which can result in a larger deduction by pooling income, wages, and property from multiple sources.

- Identify related businesses that may benefit from aggregation, especially if they share common ownership, operations, or resources.

- Make sure your businesses meet the IRS criteria for aggregation, such as centralized management or operational interdependence.

- File the appropriate documentation with the IRS to elect aggregation, and review this election annually to ensure it continues to benefit your tax situation.

- Track the combined income, wages, and property of aggregated businesses to ensure accurate reporting.

6. Get Help from a Tax Professional

The QBID rules can be complicated, and working with a tax expert can help you navigate them successfully. A professional can identify opportunities you might miss and ensure compliance with all IRS regulations.

- Meet with a tax advisor early in the year to plan your strategy for maximizing QBID.
- Seek advice on managing income thresholds, optimizing wages, and using aggregation rules.
- Stay updated on changes to tax laws with the help of your advisor, as these changes can affect your QBID eligibility or calculation.
- Ensure your tax filings are accurate and timely to avoid penalties and make the most of your deductions.
- Use your advisor's expertise to create a long-term tax strategy that integrates QBID planning with other financial goals.

7. Review Your Deduction Each Year

The factors affecting your QBID can change every year due to shifts in income, payroll, or property ownership. Annual reviews ensure you're taking full advantage of this deduction.

- Schedule yearly tax planning sessions to revisit your QBID strategy and adjust as needed.

- Review your income, expenses, and payroll records to identify any discrepancies or new opportunities.

- Stay informed about updates to tax laws, income thresholds, and QBID rules that might affect your eligibility or calculation.

- Compare your QBID from year to year to identify patterns or trends that could help you plan more effectively in the future.

8. Learn About Tax Planning

Understanding the basics of QBID and small business taxes can help you make better decisions and work more effectively with your tax advisor.

- Attend webinars, workshops, or seminars that explain QBID strategies and other small business tax topics in plain language.

- Use online resources, books, or guides to expand your knowledge of tax planning and deductions.

- Experiment with tax planning tools and software to model different scenarios and understand how changes in your income or expenses affect your QBID.

- Follow IRS updates or subscribe to newsletters from trusted tax professionals to stay informed about changes to tax laws and best practices.

- Share your knowledge with employees or business partners to ensure everyone involved in financial decision-making understands how to support your QBID strategy.

By following these steps, you can make the most of your Qualified Business Income Deduction, save money on taxes, and reinvest your savings into your business and personal goals. Careful planning and staying informed will help you take full advantage of this valuable tax benefit.

Chapter 14: How Can I Estimate My Quarterly Tax Payments Accurately?

Section 1: Why Quarterly Payments Matter

Quarterly tax payments are a key part of managing your small business finances. They help you meet your tax obligations, avoid extra costs, and ensure you're complying with government regulations. Beyond meeting legal requirements, making these payments regularly can teach you smart financial habits that benefit your business for years to come. Let's take a deeper look at why quarterly payments matter and how they can help your business thrive.

Avoiding Penalties

The U.S. tax system is based on a pay-as-you-go approach. This means you're expected to pay taxes on the money you earn throughout the year. For small business owners, freelancers, and independent contractors, this usually means making estimated quarterly payments. If you skip these payments or don't pay enough, you could face penalties from the IRS. These penalties often add up quickly and can be a significant percentage of the taxes you owe.

In addition to penalties, underpaying your taxes can lead to interest charges on the unpaid balance. Over time, these extra charges can add up, making it even harder to get caught up on your taxes. By staying on top of your quarterly payments, you can avoid these unnecessary costs and keep your finances in good shape. Paying on time also gives you peace of mind, knowing you won't face surprise fees or interest later.

It's also worth noting that penalties for missing payments aren't just financial. Falling behind on taxes can put you on the IRS's radar, increasing your chances of being audited. By staying current with your quarterly payments, you reduce this risk and show the IRS that you're a responsible taxpayer.

Managing Cash Flow

Quarterly tax payments help you spread out your tax responsibilities throughout the year, making it easier to manage your cash flow. Instead of facing one large tax bill in April, you can divide your payments into smaller, manageable amounts. This approach reduces stress and helps you plan your finances more effectively.

Setting aside money for taxes on a regular basis also encourages better budgeting. It ensures that you always have funds available to meet your obligations. This habit is especially important for businesses with fluctuating income. When your earnings vary from month to month, planning ahead for taxes can prevent financial surprises that could disrupt your operations.

In addition, maintaining steady tax payments can make your business more attractive to lenders and investors. Showing that you're financially responsible builds trust and confidence in your ability to manage money. It's not just about taxes—it's about demonstrating that your business is stable and reliable.

Staying Compliant

Compliance with tax rules is essential for the health and reputation of your business. Paying quarterly taxes on time shows the IRS that you're fulfilling your obligations, which can reduce your chances of being audited or facing legal trouble. When you consistently pay your taxes on time and in full, it signals to tax authorities that you're running your business responsibly.

Some states also have their own quarterly tax requirements. Staying on top of these payments ensures you're compliant at both the federal and state levels. Missing payments or falling behind can lead to more than just fines. It can damage your business's reputation and make customers, partners, and other stakeholders question your reliability.

Being compliant also helps you build strong relationships with your financial advisors and tax professionals. When they see that you're organized and proactive, they can provide better advice and support to help your business succeed.

Building Financial Awareness

Paying quarterly taxes requires you to stay informed about your income, expenses, and overall profitability. This process encourages you to regularly review your financial performance, helping you spot patterns and make better decisions for your business.

By taking a closer look at your finances each quarter, you're more likely to identify opportunities for growth or areas where you can save money. For example, you might discover new deductions you can claim, or you might decide to reorganize your expenses to reduce your taxable income. Regular financial check-ins also help you align your tax strategy with your business goals, ensuring you're making the most of your resources.

Over time, building this financial awareness can lead to better money management. You'll develop habits that make it easier to plan for the future, avoid unnecessary expenses, and invest in opportunities that support your business's growth. Financial awareness isn't just about paying taxes on time—it's about creating a solid foundation for long-term success.

Another benefit of staying aware of your tax situation is that it helps you prepare for unexpected changes. Whether it's a sudden drop in income or an unexpected expense, being in tune with your finances allows you to adapt more quickly and effectively. By staying proactive, you'll be better equipped to handle challenges and keep your business on track.

Encouraging Business Growth

Quarterly tax payments don't just keep you compliant— they also help you plan for the future. When you know your tax obligations in advance, you can set realistic financial goals and allocate resources more effectively. This foresight helps you avoid surprises that could derail your progress and allows you to focus on growing your business.

By staying on top of your tax payments, you're also more likely to attract opportunities for growth. Investors and partners want to work with businesses that are organized and financially stable. When you show that you're responsible with your taxes, it builds confidence in your ability to manage other aspects of your business as well.

In summary, quarterly tax payments are more than just a legal requirement. They're a practical tool for managing your finances, staying compliant, and building a strong foundation for your business. They help you avoid penalties, manage cash flow, and plan for the future, all while encouraging habits that support long-term success. In the next sections, we'll dive into how to calculate and pay your quarterly taxes and explore tools to make the process easier.

Section 2: How to Calculate and Pay Them

Paying your quarterly taxes is important to avoid penalties, interest charges, and financial problems. Here's an easy step-by-step guide to help you calculate and pay these taxes correctly:

Step 1: Know Your Taxable Income

First, figure out how much money you expect to make this year. This is your taxable income. It includes all the money your business brings in minus any business expenses you can deduct. If you're self-employed or part of a partnership or S-Corp, this will usually be your net profit. Don't forget to include other sources of income, like money from investments, rental properties, or side jobs.

Your income may change during the year, so it's smart to check your numbers regularly. Tools like spreadsheets or accounting software can help you track your income and expenses.

Step 2: Figure Out Your Taxes

To estimate your federal taxes, use this formula:

(Taxable Income) x (Estimated Tax Rate) = Federal Tax Owed

Your tax rate depends on your filing status and how much you earn. Check the latest tax brackets from the IRS to find out your rate. If you're self-employed, you also need to add self-employment taxes. These taxes pay for Social Security and Medicare. As of 2024, the self-employment tax is 15.3% of 92.35% of your net earnings.

Example: If you earn $50,000:

$50,000 x 92.35% = $46,175 (earnings taxed for self-employment)
$46,175 x 15.3% = $7,061.78 (self-employment tax)

Add this amount to your regular income taxes. For example, if your income tax is $6,000, your total tax owed will be $13,061.78.

Step 3: Use Credits and Deductions

Tax credits and deductions can lower how much you owe. Tax credits subtract directly from your taxes, while deductions reduce the income you're taxed on. Examples of credits include the Earned Income Tax Credit and Child Tax Credit. Common deductions include home office expenses, retirement contributions, and vehicle costs.

To make sure you're using all the credits and deductions you qualify for, keep up with tax law changes or talk to a tax professional.

Step 4: Split into Four Payments

Quarterly taxes are due four times a year. Take the total tax amount you calculated and divide it by four. For example, if you owe $20,000, you'll pay $5,000 each quarter.

Keep an eye on your income throughout the year. If you start earning more, adjust your payments so you don't underpay and risk penalties.

Step 5: Follow Safe Harbor Rules

To avoid penalties, make sure your payments meet one of these safe harbor rules:

1. Pay at least 90% of what you'll owe this year.
2. Pay 100% of last year's taxes (or 110% if your adjusted gross income was more than $150,000).

These rules protect you from penalties, even if you owe more taxes when you file your return.

Step 6: Pay on Time

Quarterly payments are due on these dates:

- **1st Quarter:** April 15
- **2nd Quarter:** June 15
- **3rd Quarter:** September 15
- **4th Quarter:** January 15 of the next year

If a due date falls on a weekend or holiday, the deadline moves to the next business day. Set reminders or mark your calendar to avoid late payments, which come with fees and interest.

Step 7: Make Your Payment

There are several ways to pay your taxes:

- **EFTPS (Electronic Federal Tax Payment System):** Free and secure. You can also schedule payments ahead of time.
- **IRS Direct Pay:** Lets you pay directly from your bank account with no fees.
- **Credit or Debit Card:** Easy to use but usually has a small fee.
- **Mail:** Send Form 1040-ES along with a check or money order to the IRS. Include your Social Security Number or Employer ID Number, the tax year, and the payment quarter on the check. Make sure it's postmarked by the due date.

Some states also require quarterly tax payments. Check with your state's tax office to learn their rules and how to pay.

Step 8: Keep Good Records

Stay organized by keeping track of all your income, expenses, deductions, credits, and payments. Use bookkeeping software or a simple spreadsheet to record everything. These records will make it easier to file your taxes at the end of the year and help you if the IRS ever asks questions about your payments.

Extra Tips for Success

- **Check Your Numbers Often:** Review your income and expenses each quarter. If something changes, update your tax estimates so you don't overpay or underpay.

- **Use Tax Software:** Tax software can calculate your payments and remind you about deadlines.

- **Ask for Help:** If your income is unpredictable or your taxes seem complicated, hire a tax professional to create a plan that fits your needs.

By following these steps, you can handle your quarterly taxes with confidence, avoid penalties, and keep your finances on track.

Section 3: Tools for Tracking Tax Liabilities

Estimating and paying your quarterly taxes can seem overwhelming, but the right tools can make a huge difference. With the right technology and resources, you can simplify the process, stay organized, and avoid costly mistakes. Below, we explore several effective tools and methods to help you keep track of your income, expenses, and tax payments.

1. Bookkeeping Software

Bookkeeping software is one of the best ways to track your tax obligations and stay on top of your finances. Popular tools like QuickBooks, Xero, and Wave provide easy-to-use platforms for managing your business's income and expenses. These programs can:

- Automatically categorize transactions, saving you time and reducing errors.

- Generate detailed reports like profit and loss statements, balance sheets, and cash flow summaries.

- Estimate quarterly tax payments based on your real-time financial data.

Some advanced bookkeeping tools also allow you to track payroll and inventory, offering a complete financial overview. Many programs integrate with your bank account and other financial apps, ensuring your records are always up to date. Staying organized with bookkeeping software helps you avoid last-minute scrambling and reduces the guesswork in calculating your taxes.

2. Tax Preparation Software

Tax preparation software, such as TurboTax, TaxAct, and H&R Block, is specifically designed to help individuals and small business owners manage their taxes. These tools include features tailored for estimating and filing quarterly taxes, such as:

- Built-in calculators that use your financial data to estimate your tax liabilities accurately.

- Automated reminders for key deadlines to ensure you never miss a payment.

- Integration with bookkeeping software to easily import income and expense data.

- Simulation tools to analyze how deductions and other financial decisions may impact your taxes.

Many tax preparation programs offer additional services, such as live consultations with tax professionals and audit support. This combination of automation and expert guidance can make filing quarterly taxes much less stressful.

3. IRS Direct Pay and EFTPS

The IRS provides two secure online platforms for making tax payments:

- **IRS Direct Pay:** This tool allows you to make one-time payments directly from your checking or savings account without creating an account. It provides immediate confirmation receipts for added peace of mind.

- **Electronic Federal Tax Payment System (EFTPS):** A more robust option for businesses, EFTPS lets you schedule recurring payments, track payment history, and manage multiple payment accounts. It's particularly useful for businesses with ongoing tax obligations.

Both tools are free, secure, and more efficient than mailing checks. Using these systems ensures your payments are processed quickly and accurately.

4. Spreadsheets

For those who prefer a hands-on approach, spreadsheets can be an excellent way to track your tax information. Programs like Microsoft Excel or Google Sheets allow you to create customizable templates that suit your business needs. With spreadsheets, you can:

- Record income and expenses in an organized format.
- Calculate estimated taxes based on your tax bracket and deductions.
- Keep a detailed record of your quarterly payments and track due dates.

Spreadsheets also provide flexibility to create charts, graphs, or other visuals to help you better understand your financial data. Free templates are widely available online, making this a practical and cost-effective choice for small business owners.

5. Apps for Self-Employed Individuals

Mobile apps like QuickBooks Self-Employed, TaxSlayer, and Keeper Tax are designed specifically for freelancers and small business owners. These apps are user-friendly and packed with features to make tax management simple, including:

- Automatic tracking of mileage for tax deductions.
- Real-time categorization of income and expenses, so you always know where you stand financially.
- Alerts and reminders for upcoming tax deadlines.
- Integration with other financial tools to streamline your workflow.

These apps are particularly useful for busy individuals who need to manage their taxes on the go. Many of them offer free trials or affordable subscription plans, making them accessible to a wide range of users.

6. Consultation with a Tax Professional

While software and apps can simplify tax management, consulting a tax professional can provide added accuracy and peace of mind. Tax professionals bring expertise and personalized advice that can be invaluable for small business owners. They can:

- Use advanced tools to calculate your tax payments, even if your income varies throughout the year.
- Help you adjust your estimates when your financial situation changes, such as during business growth or unexpected expenses.

- Identify deductions, credits, and other opportunities to minimize your tax liability.
- Ensure compliance with IRS regulations and reduce the risk of errors or audits.

Combining the knowledge of a tax professional with digital tools ensures you're managing your taxes effectively and not paying more than necessary.

Conclusion

Managing quarterly taxes doesn't have to be stressful. By using the right tools and resources, you can stay organized, save time, and avoid penalties. Whether you choose bookkeeping software, tax preparation programs, mobile apps, or spreadsheets, there are solutions available to fit your preferences and budget. For added confidence, consider working with a tax professional to refine your strategy. Staying proactive with these tools will let you focus on growing your business while staying compliant with tax laws.

Chapter 15: What Are the Key Tax Deadlines I Need to Know?

Section 1: Annual, Quarterly, and Special Deadlines

For small business owners, staying on top of tax deadlines is important to avoid fines, follow the rules, and keep your business running smoothly. Knowing the key dates for annual, quarterly, and special tax filings can make a big difference. This section gives a simple guide to these deadlines so you can be ready to meet them.

Annual Tax Deadlines

1. Federal Income Tax Filing
    - For most sole proprietors and single-member LLCs: April 15th is the standard deadline. This date is when you report your business earnings and claim deductions for the past year.
    - For partnerships and S-corporations: March 15th is the due date for filing returns or extensions using Form 1065 or 1120-S.
    - For C-corporations: April 15th, unless your fiscal year is different from the calendar year. In that case, your deadline is the 15th day of the fourth month after your fiscal year ends.

2. State Income Tax Filing
    - Many states have the same deadlines as federal taxes, but some may be earlier or have extra forms. Check your state's tax website to make sure you're on track. Missing state deadlines can bring penalties.
3. Annual Payroll Reports
    - Employers must send W-2 forms to employees and Form 1099-NEC to independent contractors by January 31st to report income paid during the year.
    - Additionally, Form 940 for Federal Unemployment Tax (FUTA) must also be filed by January 31st. Filing on time avoids issues with the IRS.

Quarterly Tax Deadlines

1. Estimated Tax Payments
    - If you're self-employed, own a business, or don't withhold taxes through payroll, you need to pay estimated taxes quarterly. This is required if you expect to owe more than $1,000 in taxes for the year.
    - Due dates:
        - April 15th (for income earned January 1 – March 31)

- June 15th (for income earned April 1 – May 31)
- September 15th (for income earned June 1 – August 31)
- January 15th of the next year (for income earned September 1 – December 31)
    - Paying on time helps you avoid extra fees or interest.
2. Payroll Tax Deposits
    - Employers must collect and pay federal income taxes, Social Security, and Medicare taxes. How often you pay—either semi-weekly or monthly—depends on the size of your payroll. Check the IRS rules to figure out your schedule.
    - Quarterly filings through Form 941 (Quarterly Payroll Tax Return) are due:
        - April 30th (for Q1), July 31st (for Q2), October 31st (for Q3), and January 31st (for Q4).
3. State Estimated Taxes
    - States with income taxes usually require quarterly payments like federal taxes, but details and methods can vary. Missing state payments could result in extra fees or interest.

Special Deadlines

1. Sales Tax Filings

    - Businesses that collect sales tax must send it to the correct state agency. How often you file—monthly, quarterly, or annually—depends on how much you collect. Many states set the deadline for monthly filers as the 20th of the next month (e.g., February 20th for January sales). Missing sales tax deadlines can lead to big fines.

2. Excise Tax Payments

    - Businesses in industries like alcohol, tobacco, or fuel have special tax requirements. Form 720 (Quarterly Federal Excise Tax Return) is due on the last day of the month after each quarter ends (e.g., April 30th for Q1). Know your industry's rules to stay on track.

3. Cryptocurrency Transactions

    - The IRS treats cryptocurrency like property, so gains and losses are taxable. If you've used cryptocurrency, you need to report it using Schedule D and Form 8949. Keep good records of purchase and sale dates, amounts, and values to avoid problems with the IRS.

4. Extensions
    - If you can't meet a deadline, you can ask for more time to file. Use Form 4868 (for individuals) or Form 7004 (for businesses) to get a six-month extension. For example, this moves the April 15th deadline to October 15th for individuals and to September 15th for partnerships and S-corporations. Even with an extension, you must pay any estimated taxes by the original deadline to avoid fines.

5. Industry-Specific Deadlines
    - Some businesses, like nonprofits and trusts, have unique deadlines. For example, nonprofits with a calendar-year fiscal year file Form 990 by May 15th. Talk to a tax expert to learn the deadlines that apply to your business type.

By keeping these deadlines in mind, you can stay ahead of your tax responsibilities, avoid penalties, and focus on running your business. The next section will share tips for staying organized and meeting these deadlines on time

Section 2: Strategies for Staying Compliant

Keeping up with tax deadlines is important for small business owners to avoid fines, extra fees, and unnecessary stress. Here are some simple ways to make sure you're on top of your tax responsibilities and protecting your business:

1. Keep Accurate Records

Good record-keeping is key to staying on top of your taxes. Make sure to keep track of all income, expenses, and other financial activities. Using bookkeeping software can save time by organizing and recording everything automatically. Check your accounts every month to keep them up-to-date and correct.

Also, keep physical and digital copies of receipts, invoices, and other documents in clearly marked folders. Having everything organized will make it easier to handle tax preparation and audits.

2. Make a Tax Calendar

A tax calendar helps you keep track of when payments and forms are due. Include dates for:

- Quarterly estimated tax payments.
- Annual tax returns.
- Payroll tax filings.
- Sales tax payments.

Set reminders well before these deadlines to give yourself plenty of time to prepare. Use different colors or markers to highlight the most important dates. You can also use apps or online tools to sync this calendar with your phone or computer.

Coordinate your tax calendar with your business plans to make sure you have the money ready when taxes are due. This way, you avoid surprises or last-minute problems.

3. Work with a Tax Professional

A tax professional, like a CPA or Enrolled Agent, can be a big help. They can:

- Explain your specific tax responsibilities.
- File your taxes correctly and on time.
- Keep you updated on any changes to tax laws.

If your business deals with things like multi-state taxes or cryptocurrency, a tax expert's advice becomes even more important. They can also help you find ways to save money through deductions and credits.

Plan to meet with your tax advisor several times a year, not just at tax time. This will help you stay prepared for changes in your business or tax laws.

4. Separate Business and Personal Finances

Mixing your personal and business money can make taxes messy. Use a different bank account and credit card just for your business. This makes it easier to track and report your business expenses.

Keep your business accounts for business purposes only. Don't use them for personal expenses unless you're taking an owner's draw or salary, depending on your business setup. This keeps things clear and avoids confusion during tax season.

5. Save Money for Taxes

Don't get caught short when taxes are due. Set aside a portion of your income regularly to cover estimated payments. Open a separate savings account just for taxes and add to it throughout the year.

Decide how much to save based on your expected taxes and income level. Some business owners set aside 25% to 30% of their revenue. Setting up automatic transfers can help you stay on track.

6. Use Accounting and Tax Tools

Technology can make handling taxes much easier. Many bookkeeping programs work with tax software to:

- Track expenses that are deductible.
- Calculate estimated taxes.
- Create forms like 1099s or W-2s.

Popular tools include QuickBooks, Xero, TurboTax, and TaxAct. If you have employees, consider software that combines payroll and tax filing to save even more time.

Look for software with features like automatic expense categorization, real-time tax estimates, and shared access for your team or accountant. These tools can save you time, reduce mistakes, and make tax compliance easier.

7. Stay Updated on Tax Laws

Tax rules change often, so it's important to stay informed. Sign up for newsletters from the IRS or your state's tax agency. Webinars, workshops, or updates from your tax advisor can also keep you in the loop.

You might also join business groups or professional associations that share tax information. Knowing the latest rules helps you stay compliant and take advantage of new tax benefits.

8. Prepare for Special Deadlines

Some businesses have extra tax requirements, like excise taxes or international reporting. Plan ahead for these deadlines by using a checklist specific to your industry.

Review your business regularly to see if new tax rules apply. For example, expanding your business to new states or offering new services might create additional tax responsibilities. Staying ahead of these changes keeps things running smoothly.

9. Check In Regularly

Take time every few months to review your finances and tax progress. This helps you see if you're on track with estimated payments and if anything has changed in your business that might affect your taxes.

Talk with your bookkeeper or accountant during these check-ins to fix any problems early and plan for the future. Regular reviews help you avoid surprises and keep your finances healthy.

10. Act Fast if There's a Problem

If you miss a deadline or get a notice from the IRS, don't ignore it. File late returns, pay fines, or set up a payment plan as soon as possible to prevent further issues. Delaying can lead to bigger penalties or legal trouble.

Reach out to the IRS or your tax professional for help. Taking quick action shows responsibility and can sometimes result in reduced fines or easier payment options.

By using these strategies, you can meet your tax responsibilities, avoid penalties, and keep your business running smoothly. A little planning and organization go a long way toward making tax season less stressful.

Chapter 16: How Do I Collect and Remit Sales Tax for My Business?

Section 1: Overview of Sales Tax Laws

Sales tax is a type of tax charged by state and local governments on the sale of goods and some services. It's usually a percentage of the sale price and is added when a customer makes a purchase. Business owners need to understand the rules about sales tax to stay compliant and avoid fines. This section explains how sales tax works, what it covers, and what business owners are responsible for.

What Is Sales Tax?

Sales tax is a tax on items or services that are sold. The customer pays the tax at checkout, and the business collects it and sends it to the government. The amount of sales tax depends on where the sale happens—different states, counties, and cities may have their own tax rates. Some places charge the same rate across the whole state, while others let local areas add extra taxes. In some cases, there may be special taxes for specific items, like alcohol or tobacco products.

Sales tax serves as a significant source of revenue for state and local governments. It helps fund schools, public transportation, emergency services, and other community programs. For business owners, understanding sales tax is not just about compliance—it's also about contributing to the local economy and maintaining trust with customers.

Taxable Goods and Services

Each state has its own rules about what is taxed. Most of the time, physical items like clothes, electronics, and furniture are taxable, but many services are not. However, in some states, specific services like repairs, cleaning, or entertainment are taxed. Digital products like e-books, music downloads, and video streaming services might also be taxed, depending on the state. With the rise of e-commerce and digital subscriptions, states are increasingly looking to tax digital goods and services to keep up with changing consumer habits.

Businesses must carefully determine which of their products or services are taxable. For example, a business selling software might need to charge sales tax on boxed software but not on custom-built programs or cloud-based solutions. Bundled goods and services can create additional complexity, as businesses may need to separate taxable and non-taxable items in the bundle.

Understanding what is taxable requires thorough research and possibly consulting with a tax professional. Misclassifying goods or services can lead to underpayment or overpayment of taxes, both of which can be costly.

Nexus: Establishing a Connection

Nexus is a term that means a business has a connection to a state. If your business has nexus in a state, you must collect and pay sales tax there. Nexus can happen in several ways:

- **Physical Presence:** If your business has a store, office, warehouse, or employees in a state, you likely have nexus there. Even temporary activities like setting up a booth at a trade show or having traveling sales representatives can create nexus.

- **Economic Nexus:** If your sales or the number of transactions in a state go over a certain limit, you might have nexus even if you don't have a physical presence. For example, many states set thresholds such as $100,000 in sales or 200 transactions in a year.

- **Affiliate Nexus:** Working with partners or affiliates in a state can also create nexus. This happens when an affiliate helps promote or sell your products within the state.

- **Marketplace Facilitators:** Online platforms like Amazon, Etsy, and eBay often collect sales tax on behalf of sellers. However, sellers still need to ensure that these platforms are handling sales tax correctly and may need to report sales separately.

Knowing where your business has nexus is critical. Ignoring nexus obligations can lead to fines, back taxes, and interest charges, so it's essential to regularly review where your business operates or sells.

Sales Tax Exemptions

Some items, services, or buyers don't have to pay sales tax. Common exemptions include:

- **Resale Exemption:** If someone buys goods to resell, they don't have to pay sales tax. The buyer must provide the seller with a valid resale certificate to prove the purchase is for resale.

- **Nonprofit Organizations:** Groups like schools, churches, or charities often don't have to pay sales tax. However, these organizations usually need to apply for an exemption and provide documentation to sellers.

- **Essential Goods:** Necessities like groceries, prescription medicines, and some medical devices are often exempt from sales tax. However, what qualifies as "essential" varies by state. For example, some states tax soda or candy even if groceries are tax-free.

Businesses must keep accurate records of exemptions, including certificates or other proof, in case of an audit. Misusing exemptions or failing to document them properly can result in penalties.

Compliance and Penalties

If a business doesn't collect or pay sales tax correctly, it can face fines, interest, and audits. Here are some key responsibilities:

- **Register for a Sales Tax Permit:** Businesses must register for a sales tax permit in every state where they have nexus. Most states offer online registration systems that make this process straightforward.

- **Collect Sales Tax:** Businesses must charge the correct sales tax rate on taxable items or services. This includes accounting for state, county, and city rates. Many businesses use point-of-sale systems or tax software to calculate sales tax automatically.

- **File Sales Tax Returns:** Businesses must regularly file sales tax returns and pay the taxes they've collected. Filing frequency depends on the state and the amount of sales tax collected. Late filings can result in penalties and interest.

Keeping up with sales tax laws can be challenging. States frequently change tax rates, expand the list of taxable items, or adjust nexus thresholds. For example, some states may start taxing new categories of digital goods or implement stricter rules for marketplace facilitators.

Audits are a common way states ensure businesses follow sales tax laws. During an audit, the state may review records like invoices, exemption certificates, and sales tax returns. Organized and accurate records make the process smoother and reduce the likelihood of penalties. Businesses should keep these records for at least three to five years, depending on state requirements.

By understanding sales tax rules, keeping detailed records, and using tools like tax software, businesses can avoid compliance issues and focus on growth. Consulting a tax professional can also provide valuable guidance, especially for businesses operating in multiple states or dealing with complex transactions.

Section 2: How to Register, Collect, and Pay Sales Tax

Paying sales tax is an important part of running a business that sells goods or services. Following the rules not only helps you avoid fines but also builds trust with customers and keeps your business compliant. Here is an expanded, step-by-step guide to ensure you handle sales tax correctly:

Step 1: Find Out if You Need to Collect Sales Tax

Before collecting sales tax, determine whether your business has a "nexus" in a state. Nexus means a connection or presence that requires you to collect sales tax. This could include:

- **Physical presence:** Having a store, office, or warehouse in the state.
- **Employees or contractors:** Workers operating in the state on behalf of your business.
- **Temporary activities:** Participating in trade shows, pop-up shops, or other events.
- **Economic thresholds:** Many states have specific rules, such as requiring sales tax collection if you exceed $100,000 in sales or 200 transactions within a year.

It's crucial to research the rules on the state's Department of Revenue website to confirm if your business qualifies. Failing to comply with nexus requirements can result in penalties and back taxes.

Step 2: Register for a Sales Tax Permit

If you determine that your business needs to collect sales tax in a state, you must register for a sales tax permit before making any taxable sales. Here's what to do:

1. **Visit the state's tax website:** Locate the application form for a sales tax permit.
2. **Provide accurate information:** You'll need to submit details like:
    - Your business name and structure (e.g., sole proprietorship, LLC, corporation).
    - Your EIN (Employer Identification Number).
    - Business addresses (physical, mailing, and any additional locations).
    - A description of the goods or services you sell, including any that may be exempt.
3. **Pay any fees:** While some states issue permits for free, others charge a nominal fee. Check the specific requirements for each state.
4. **Receive your permit number:** Keep this number handy for invoices, receipts, and tax filings to confirm your compliance with state laws.

Step 3: Charge the Correct Sales Tax Rate

Sales tax rates can vary widely, depending on where the sale takes place. It's essential to calculate the correct rate every time you make a sale. Here's how:

- **Understand state and local tax rates:** States set base tax rates, but additional local taxes (from cities, counties, or districts) may apply.

- **Know sourcing rules:**

    - **Origin-based sourcing:** Sales tax is based on your business's location.

    - **Destination-based sourcing:** Sales tax is based on the buyer's location.

- **Leverage tools:** Software like QuickBooks or Avalara can automatically calculate the appropriate tax rate based on the customer's address.

Double-check which of your products or services are taxable, as exemptions may apply to items like groceries, clothing, or prescription medications in some states.

Step 4: Keep Detailed Records of Sales and Taxes

Keeping accurate and detailed records is crucial for managing sales tax and preparing for potential audits. Track:

- **Total sales:** Record every transaction, including taxable and non-taxable sales.

- **Sales tax collected:** Document the tax collected for each jurisdiction to ensure accuracy.
- **Exempt sales:** Retain exemption certificates and any supporting documentation for sales that didn't include tax.

Using reliable accounting software can simplify record-keeping, reduce errors, and help you generate reports when it's time to file taxes.

Step 5: File Sales Tax Returns

Every state where you're registered to collect sales tax requires you to file regular returns, even if you didn't collect any tax during the period. Here's how to stay on track:

1. **Understand your filing frequency:** States assign filing schedules—monthly, quarterly, or annually—based on your business's sales volume.
2. **Prepare your return:**
    - Report total sales, taxable sales, and tax collected.
    - Deduct any non-taxable or exempt sales.
    - Calculate the amount owed based on your records.
3. **Submit your return online:** Most states require electronic filing through their tax portals, which makes the process quicker and reduces the chance of errors.

Step 6: Pay the Tax You Collected

After submitting your return, you need to remit the tax collected to the state. Follow these tips to ensure smooth payments:

- **Use electronic payment methods:** Many states require electronic payments to process taxes efficiently.
- **Stick to deadlines:** Missing a payment deadline can result in penalties and interest charges, so mark your calendar for due dates.

Step 7: Handle Exempt Sales Correctly

Not every sale requires sales tax. If you sell to tax-exempt buyers, like wholesalers or nonprofits, follow these steps:

- **Collect exemption certificates:** Buyers must provide a valid exemption or resale certificate. Ensure the certificate is complete and current.
- **Verify the information:** Double-check that the buyer's details match state requirements.
- **Keep records:** Store these certificates securely as proof during audits.

Understanding exemption rules for each state helps prevent errors and protects your business from fines.

Step 8: Stay Up-to-Date on Sales Tax Laws

Sales tax laws frequently change, and staying informed is vital to remain compliant. Here's how to keep up:

- **Subscribe to updates:** Sign up for email notifications or newsletters from state tax agencies.

- **Invest in professional advice:** Tax professionals or consultants can help you navigate complex rules and provide tailored guidance.

- **Use advanced tools:** Many tax software platforms automatically update to reflect changes in rates, thresholds, and regulations.

Step 9: Plan for Audits

Sales tax audits can happen at any time, so being prepared is crucial. Ensure your records are well-organized and include:

- Sales and tax collection data.
- Exemption certificates.
- Copies of filed returns.

Regularly review your records for accuracy and completeness to minimize stress during an audit.

Final Thoughts

By following these expanded steps, you can simplify the process of registering, collecting, and paying sales tax. Setting up efficient systems, using helpful tools, and staying informed about the latest rules will help you avoid mistakes and focus on growing your business. Remember, sales tax compliance isn't just a legal requirement—it's an important part of building trust with your customers and maintaining your business's reputation.

Section 3: State-Specific Considerations

Understanding state-specific sales tax requirements can be simplified with an informational table that outlines the key considerations for each state. Below is a summary table:

State	Nexus Requirements	Taxable Goods/Services	Local Sales Tax Rules	Filing Frequency	Exemptions/Resale Certificates	Compliance Tools
Alabama	Physical/Economic Nexus	Tangible property, some services	Destination-based sourcing	Monthly/Quarterly/Annually	Nonprofits, interstate commerce, resale	Online portal, rate lookup tool
Alaska	Physical Nexus only	No state sales tax; local taxes apply	Varies by jurisdiction	Varies by jurisdiction	Not applicable	Local jurisdiction tools
Arizona	Physical/Economic Nexus	Tangible property, some digital goods	Destination-based sourcing	Monthly/Quarterly	Resale certificates	Online portal, webinars
Arkansas	Physical/Economic Nexus	Tangible property, most services	Destination-based sourcing	Monthly/Quarterly/Annually	Nonprofits, resale certificates	Online portal, rate lookup tool
California	Physical/Economic Nexus	Tangible property, some digital goods	Destination-based sourcing	Monthly/Quarterly	Resale certificates	Online portal, educational materials
Colorado	Physical/Economic Nexus	Tangible property, most services	Destination-based sourcing	Monthly/Quarterly/Annually	Nonprofits, resale certificates	Online portal, webinars
Connecticut	Physical/Economic Nexus	Tangible property, digital goods	Destination-based sourcing	Monthly/Quarterly	Nonprofits, resale certificates	Online portal, webinars

State	Nexus	Taxable Items	Sourcing	Filing Frequency	Exemptions	Resources
Delaware	No state sales tax	Not applicable	Not applicable	Not applicable	Not applicable	Not applicable
Florida	Physical/Economic Nexus	Tangible property, some services	Destination-based sourcing	Monthly/Quarterly	Nonprofits, resale certificates	Online portal, educational materials
Georgia	Physical/Economic Nexus	Tangible property, digital goods	Destination-based sourcing	Monthly/Quarterly	Nonprofits, resale certificates	Online portal, rate lookup tool
Hawaii	Physical/Economic Nexus	General excise tax instead of sales tax	Destination-based sourcing	Monthly/Quarterly	Nonprofits, resale certificates	Online portal, webinars
Idaho	Physical/Economic Nexus	Tangible property, some services	Destination-based sourcing	Monthly/Quarterly	Nonprofits, resale certificates	Online portal, rate lookup tool
Illinois	Physical/Economic Nexus	Tangible property, digital goods	Destination-based sourcing	Monthly/Quarterly	Nonprofits, resale certificates	Online portal, educational materials
Indiana	Physical/Economic Nexus	Tangible property, some digital goods	Destination-based sourcing	Monthly/Quarterly	Nonprofits, resale certificates	Online portal, webinars
Iowa	Physical/Economic Nexus	Tangible property, some services	Destination-based sourcing	Monthly/Quarterly	Nonprofits, resale certificates	Online portal, rate lookup tool
Kansas	Physical/Economic Nexus	Tangible property, some digital goods	Destination-based sourcing	Monthly/Quarterly	Nonprofits, resale certificates	Online portal, webinars
Kentucky	Physical/Economic Nexus	Tangible property, some services	Destination-based sourcing	Monthly/Quarterly	Nonprofits, resale certificates	Online portal, rate lookup tool
Louisiana	Physical/Economic Nexus	Tangible property, most services	Destination-based sourcing	Monthly/Quarterly	Nonprofits, resale certificates	Online portal, webinars

State	Nexus	Taxable	Sourcing	Filing Frequency	Exemptions	Resources
Maine	Physical/Economic Nexus	Tangible property, some services	Destination-based sourcing	Monthly/Quarterly	Nonprofits, resale certificates	Online portal, rate lookup tool
Maryland	Physical/Economic Nexus	Tangible property, digital goods	Destination-based sourcing	Monthly/Quarterly	Nonprofits, resale certificates	Online portal, educational materials
Massachusetts	Physical/Economic Nexus	Tangible property, some digital goods	Destination-based sourcing	Monthly/Quarterly	Nonprofits, resale certificates	Online portal, webinars
Michigan	Physical/Economic Nexus	Tangible property, some services	Destination-based sourcing	Monthly/Quarterly	Nonprofits, resale certificates	Online portal, rate lookup tool
Minnesota	Physical/Economic Nexus	Tangible property, some digital goods	Destination-based sourcing	Monthly/Quarterly	Nonprofits, resale certificates	Online portal, webinars
Mississippi	Physical/Economic Nexus	Tangible property, some services	Destination-based sourcing	Monthly/Quarterly	Nonprofits, resale certificates	Online portal, rate lookup tool
Missouri	Physical/Economic Nexus	Tangible property, some digital goods	Destination-based sourcing	Monthly/Quarterly	Nonprofits, resale certificates	Online portal, webinars
Montana	No sales tax	Not applicable	Not applicable	Not applicable	Not applicable	Not applicable
Nebraska	Physical/Economic Nexus	Tangible property, some services	Destination-based sourcing	Monthly/Quarterly	Nonprofits, resale certificates	Online portal, rate lookup tool
Nevada	Physical/Economic Nexus	Tangible property, some digital goods	Destination-based sourcing	Monthly/Quarterly	Nonprofits, resale certificates	Online portal, educational materials
New Hampshire	No state sales tax	Not applicable	Not applicable	Not applicable	Not applicable	Not applicable

State	Nexus	Taxable Items	Sourcing	Filing Frequency	Exemptions	Resources
New Jersey	Physical/Economic Nexus	Tangible property, some services	Destination-based sourcing	Monthly/Quarterly	Nonprofits, resale certificates	Online portal, rate lookup tool
New Mexico	Physical/Economic Nexus	Gross receipts tax applied to most goods	Destination-based sourcing	Monthly/Quarterly	Nonprofits, resale certificates	Online portal, educational materials
New York	Physical/Economic Nexus	Tangible property, digital goods	Destination-based sourcing	Monthly/Quarterly	Nonprofits, resale certificates	Online portal, webinars
North Carolina	Physical/Economic Nexus	Tangible property, some services	Destination-based sourcing	Monthly/Quarterly	Nonprofits, resale certificates	Online portal, rate lookup tool
North Dakota	Physical/Economic Nexus	Tangible property, some digital goods	Destination-based sourcing	Monthly/Quarterly	Nonprofits, resale certificates	Online portal, webinars
Ohio	Physical/Economic Nexus	Tangible property, some services	Destination-based sourcing	Monthly/Quarterly	Nonprofits, resale certificates	Online portal, rate lookup tool
Oklahoma	Physical/Economic Nexus	Tangible property, some digital goods	Destination-based sourcing	Monthly/Quarterly	Nonprofits, resale certificates	Online portal, webinars
Oregon	No sales tax	Not applicable	Not applicable	Not applicable	Not applicable	Not applicable
Pennsylvania	Physical/Economic Nexus	Tangible property, some services	Destination-based sourcing	Monthly/Quarterly	Nonprofits, resale certificates	Online portal, rate lookup tool
Rhode Island	Physical/Economic Nexus	Tangible property, some digital goods	Destination-based sourcing	Monthly/Quarterly	Nonprofits, resale certificates	Online portal, webinars
South Carolina	Physical/Economic Nexus	Tangible property, some services	Destination-based sourcing	Monthly/Quarterly	Nonprofits, resale certificates	Online portal, rate lookup tool

State	Nexus	Taxable items	Sourcing	Filing frequency	Exemptions	Resources
South Dakota	Physical/Economic Nexus	Tangible property, some services	Destination-based sourcing	Monthly/Quarterly	Nonprofits, resale certificates	Online portal, webinars
Tennessee	Physical/Economic Nexus	Tangible property, some digital goods	Destination-based sourcing	Monthly/Quarterly	Nonprofits, resale certificates	Online portal, rate lookup tool
Texas	Physical/Economic Nexus	Tangible property, some services	Destination-based sourcing	Monthly/Quarterly	Nonprofits, resale certificates	Online portal, educational materials
Utah	Physical/Economic Nexus	Tangible property, some services	Destination-based sourcing	Monthly/Quarterly	Nonprofits, resale certificates	Online portal, rate lookup tool
Vermont	Physical/Economic Nexus	Tangible property, digital goods	Destination-based sourcing	Monthly/Quarterly	Nonprofits, resale certificates	Online portal, webinars
Virginia	Physical/Economic Nexus	Tangible property, some services	Destination-based sourcing	Monthly/Quarterly	Nonprofits, resale certificates	Online portal, rate lookup tool
Washington	Physical/Economic Nexus	Tangible property, digital goods	Destination-based sourcing	Monthly/Quarterly	Nonprofits, resale certificates	Online portal, webinars
West Virginia	Physical/Economic Nexus	Tangible property, some services	Destination-based sourcing	Monthly/Quarterly	Nonprofits, resale certificates	Online portal, rate lookup tool
Wisconsin	Physical/Economic Nexus	Tangible property, some services	Destination-based sourcing	Monthly/Quarterly	Nonprofits, resale certificates	Online portal, webinars
Wyoming	Physical/Economic Nexus	Tangible property, some digital goods	Destination-based sourcing	Monthly/Quarterly	Nonprofits, resale certificates	Online portal, rate lookup tool

Chapter 17: How Does the IRS View Cryptocurrency Transactions for Tax Purposes?

Section 1: IRS Rules on Cryptocurrency

The Internal Revenue Service (IRS) treats cryptocurrency like property instead of money. This decision, explained in Notice 2014-21, means the tax rules for cryptocurrency are similar to those for stocks and real estate. Knowing these rules is important because not following them can lead to penalties and extra taxes. Here's a clear explanation of the IRS's main rules about cryptocurrency:

1. **Taxable Events:**

    - **Selling cryptocurrency for cash:** If you sell your cryptocurrency for U.S. dollars or other money, you need to report any profit or loss. This is based on the difference between what you sold it for and what you originally paid. Even small transactions can result in taxable events, so keeping track of all sales is critical.

    - **Trading one cryptocurrency for another:** Swapping one type of cryptocurrency, like Bitcoin, for another, like Ethereum, counts as a taxable event. The IRS uses the fair market value (FMV) of the cryptocurrency you received to figure out your profit or loss. This rule applies even if you didn't receive any cash as part of the transaction.

- **Using cryptocurrency to buy things:** If you spend cryptocurrency to purchase goods or services, it's treated as a sale. You need to calculate and report any gain or loss based on the change in value of the cryptocurrency since you got it. For example, buying a cup of coffee with Bitcoin could trigger a taxable event if the value of Bitcoin has changed since you acquired it.
- **Earning cryptocurrency as income:** If you mine, stake, or get paid in cryptocurrency, it counts as income. The FMV of the cryptocurrency on the day you received it is used to figure out how much income you earned. This income might also be subject to self-employment taxes. It's important to note that mined cryptocurrency may also carry additional tax obligations at the time of sale.

2. **Determining Cost Basis:**
   - Your cost basis is how much you paid for the cryptocurrency, including fees. For mined cryptocurrency, the FMV on the day it was mined becomes the cost basis. Keeping good records of how much you paid and when is very important, as the

IRS requires detailed documentation for every transaction.

- Certain events like airdrops or hard forks can change the cost basis. For example, if you receive free cryptocurrency from an airdrop, its FMV when you got it becomes the new basis. If the value fluctuates, accurate reporting becomes even more crucial.

- Some taxpayers may use specific identification methods to calculate their gains, such as FIFO (first-in, first-out) or LIFO (last-in, first-out). Choosing the right method can have a significant impact on your tax liability.

3. **Short-Term vs. Long-Term Gains:**

    - If you sell your cryptocurrency less than a year after buying it, any profit or loss is considered short-term and is taxed like regular income. Short-term rates can be higher, so frequent trading can lead to a larger tax bill.

    - If you hold it for more than a year before selling, you qualify for long-term capital gains rates, which are often lower and depend on your income level. This rule encourages taxpayers to hold onto their assets for longer periods to benefit from reduced tax rates.

4. **Hard Forks and Airdrops:**
    - When a cryptocurrency splits into two (hard fork) or when free tokens are distributed (airdrop), the IRS considers it income. The FMV of the new cryptocurrency at the time you receive it determines how much income you report. This rule applies even if you didn't request the new cryptocurrency or have control over the event.
    - You have to report these events, even if you didn't actively participate or request the new cryptocurrency. If you fail to do so, you could face penalties or additional scrutiny during an audit.

5. **Reporting Obligations:**
    - The IRS requires you to report all taxable cryptocurrency transactions. Usually, this means filling out Form 8949 and Schedule D for profits and losses. Income earned through cryptocurrency is reported on Schedule 1 or other forms as needed.
    - Good record-keeping is essential. This includes noting the date, FMV, purpose of the transaction, and any fees. Failing to report transactions accurately can lead to penalties, extra taxes, or even criminal charges in serious cases. Tools like

cryptocurrency tax software can help simplify the process.

6. **Foreign Account Reporting:**
    - If you keep cryptocurrency in a foreign account or wallet and the total value exceeds certain limits, you might need to report it under FBAR (Foreign Bank and Financial Accounts) or FATCA (Foreign Account Tax Compliance Act). Missing these requirements can lead to large penalties. The rules surrounding foreign-held cryptocurrency are complex and subject to change.
    - Reporting requirements for foreign accounts often depend on the total value of the assets, and different thresholds apply for FBAR and FATCA. Staying informed about these rules is important for anyone with international crypto holdings.

7. **Implications of Non-Compliance:**
    - The IRS is paying more attention to cryptocurrency users. They've sent letters to people who may not have reported their transactions and even added a question about cryptocurrency to tax forms. Not reporting taxable transactions could result in audits, fines, or criminal investigations.

- In recent years, the IRS has partnered with blockchain analytics firms to identify unreported transactions. This makes it even more important for taxpayers to stay compliant and report all relevant activity accurately.

8. **Evolving Guidance:**

    - As cryptocurrency grows, the IRS is updating its rules. For example, new areas like decentralized finance (DeFi) and non-fungible tokens (NFTs) bring unique tax challenges. Staying informed and seeking advice from tax experts is a good idea to stay compliant.

    - The IRS has also issued additional FAQs and rulings to address specific scenarios. However, some gray areas remain, particularly around staking rewards, yield farming, and DeFi platforms. Keeping up with these developments is crucial for proper tax reporting.

Understanding these rules helps you stay within the law and avoid trouble with the IRS. Cryptocurrency taxes can be complicated, especially if you trade often, mine, or use DeFi. Talking to a tax professional and keeping detailed records, possibly with specialized crypto tax software, can make the process much easier and help prevent issues if you're audited. Proper planning and organization can also reduce the stress of handling crypto taxes during tax season.

Section 2: Tracking and Reporting Cryptocurrency Transactions

Cryptocurrency transactions can make taxes tricky, but understanding the basics can make it easier. The IRS treats cryptocurrency as property, not money. This means every time you use or sell cryptocurrency, it may create a taxable event. Keeping track of these activities is crucial for staying compliant with tax laws. Here's a detailed guide to help you manage your crypto taxes efficiently.

1. What Counts as a Taxable Crypto Event?

The IRS taxes specific cryptocurrency activities. These include:

- **Selling cryptocurrency for cash (like USD):** If you sell crypto, you'll either have a gain or a loss. The amount is based on the difference between what you originally paid and how much you sold it for.

- **Trading one cryptocurrency for another:** When you trade crypto for a different cryptocurrency, it's treated like selling it for dollars. You'll need to calculate the value of the crypto at the time of the trade.

- **Using cryptocurrency to buy goods or services:** If you pay for something with crypto, it counts as a sale. You'll need to figure out whether you had a gain or loss based on how much the crypto was worth when you used it.

- **Getting paid in cryptocurrency:** If you earn crypto from mining, staking, or as payment for work, it counts as income. The value of the crypto in dollars when you receive it must be reported as taxable income.

Some activities are not taxable, such as:

- Transferring cryptocurrency between wallets you own. Be sure to keep records showing that both wallets belong to you.
- Buying cryptocurrency with cash, unless there are fees that create a gain or loss.

Understanding the difference between taxable and non-taxable events helps you avoid mistakes and ensures you stay on the right side of the law.

2. Tools to Track Your Crypto Transactions

Accurate record-keeping is the key to managing your crypto taxes. There are two main ways to track your transactions:

- **Use Crypto Tax Software:** Tools like CoinTracker, TaxBit, and Koinly connect directly to your crypto exchanges and wallets. They organize your transactions, calculate your gains and losses, and even prepare the forms you need for your taxes. Some tools can also handle decentralized finance (DeFi) and non-fungible tokens (NFTs).

- **Track Manually:** If you prefer to handle it yourself, a spreadsheet can work just as well. For each transaction, log:

    o The date and time of the transaction.

    o The type of transaction (buy, sell, trade, payment, etc.).

    o How much cryptocurrency was involved.

    o Its value in dollars at the time of the transaction.

    o Any fees you paid.

    o Your gain or loss for each transaction.

Manual tracking gives you more control but requires time and attention to detail. If you have many transactions, software can save you a lot of effort.

3. How to Report Your Transactions

Using Form 8949 and Schedule D

If you have gains or losses from cryptocurrency, you need to report them on **Form 8949**. This form details every transaction and connects to **Schedule D** of your tax return. You'll need to provide:

- The type of cryptocurrency (e.g., Bitcoin, Ethereum).

- When you bought it and when you sold or used it.

- The amount you earned or lost on each transaction.

If you have hundreds of transactions, crypto tax software can automate this process, making it much faster and easier.

Reporting Crypto Income

If you earn cryptocurrency, you'll report it as income. Here's where to include it:

- **Schedule C** if it's business income.
- **Schedule 1** for other types of income.

Use the dollar value of the cryptocurrency at the time you received it. For mining and staking rewards, this is usually the market value on the day it was credited to your account.

What About Form 1099?

Some crypto exchanges may send you a **Form 1099-B** or **Form 1099-K** to summarize your transactions. However, not all exchanges provide these forms, so don't rely solely on them. Always compare these forms with your own records to ensure accuracy.

4. DeFi and NFTs

Decentralized finance (DeFi) and non-fungible tokens (NFTs) can make crypto taxes even more complex. To stay compliant:

- Record every DeFi transaction, such as staking, lending, borrowing, or yield farming. Many of these activities create taxable events.

- For NFTs, track how much you paid for them, what you sold them for, and any fees. Treat NFT sales like other cryptocurrency transactions, reporting gains or losses accordingly.

Many tax software tools now include features to manage DeFi and NFT transactions, simplifying this process.

5. Staying Compliant with the IRS

Here are some tips to make sure you follow IRS rules:

- **Report every transaction:** Even small gains or losses need to be included on your tax return.

- **Keep your records organized:** Save transaction logs, exchange statements, and wallet activity for at least three years. If you've omitted significant income, keep records longer.

- **Stay informed about changes:** Crypto tax laws and guidelines change frequently. Check for updates from the IRS or consult a tax expert who specializes in cryptocurrency.

By using the right tools, understanding your obligations, and keeping accurate records, you can simplify the process of reporting cryptocurrency taxes. Following these steps will help you avoid penalties and give you peace of mind as you navigate the exciting but ever-changing world of cryptocurrency.

Section 3: Tax-Saving Strategies for Crypto-Related Income

Cryptocurrency transactions can have big tax impacts, but with smart planning, you can lower the amount you owe. Here are some easy-to-understand strategies for saving on crypto-related taxes, explained in more detail to give you the tools you need:

1. Learn About Holding Periods

The IRS looks at how long you keep your cryptocurrency before selling it. If you sell after one year or less, it's considered a short-term gain and taxed at higher rates, like regular income. But if you hold it for over a year, it counts as a long-term gain and gets taxed at lower rates. To save on taxes, try to hold your crypto for more than a year before selling.

Spreading out your sales over different years can also help you keep your taxable income lower. For example, if you sell part of your holdings in one year and the rest in another, you can avoid pushing yourself into a higher tax bracket. You should also keep track of when you bought your crypto and plan your sales accordingly to maximize savings.

2. Use Tax-Loss Harvesting

If you sell cryptocurrency at a loss, you can use that loss to cancel out other investment gains. This helps reduce the amount of income that gets taxed. If your losses are bigger than your gains, you can carry the extra losses into future years to reduce future taxable income.

Right now, the "wash sale rule" doesn't apply to crypto, which means you can sell your crypto at a loss and immediately buy it back to maintain your position. However, this could change, so keep an eye on new rules. Review your crypto holdings often to see where you can balance out gains and losses. Using tax software or a professional to track your transactions can make this process much easier.

3. Claim Mining and Staking Deductions

If you earn crypto by mining or staking, you can deduct costs like electricity, equipment, and repairs. Keep good records and receipts to prove these expenses. If you mine or stake as part of a business, you can deduct even more, like depreciation on equipment or office costs. If you have a special workspace just for mining, it might help you qualify for more deductions.

For example, if you're mining Bitcoin and spend a lot on electricity, you can deduct those energy costs. Similarly, if your staking activity involves fees or services, those can also reduce your taxable income. Always classify your mining or staking correctly, as a business or hobby, since this affects how much you can deduct.

4. Donate Crypto to Charities

Giving cryptocurrency to a charity can save you money in two ways: you can deduct the full value of the donation, and you won't have to pay taxes on any gains the crypto earned. Make sure the charity is qualified by the IRS, and get a receipt for your donation.

For big donations, you might need to have the value appraised. Timing your donation for the end of the year can help with tax planning while supporting a cause you care about. Plus, some charities are now equipped to accept crypto directly, which makes the process even smoother and ensures you get the full benefit of the tax deduction.

5. Use Self-Directed IRAs

A self-directed IRA lets you invest in cryptocurrency while avoiding immediate taxes. Gains in a traditional IRA are taxed later, while gains in a Roth IRA can be completely tax-free if you follow the rules.

Watch out for account fees and make sure you follow IRS rules to avoid penalties. For long-term investors, Roth IRAs are especially helpful because you can take out gains without paying taxes when you retire. By combining crypto investments with retirement planning, you can grow your wealth over time while minimizing tax liability.

6. Time Your Trades Smartly

When you sell your cryptocurrency can affect how much tax you owe. Selling in a year when your income is lower might mean you pay less in taxes. You can also match up gains and losses in the same year to lower your taxable income.

Another tip is to give crypto as a gift to family members, which may be tax-free up to a certain limit. This can also lower your taxable estate. By timing your trades and gifts carefully, you can make the most of tax-free thresholds and keep more of your earnings.

7. Use Qualified Opportunity Zones (QOZs)

If you've made a lot of money from crypto, you can reinvest those gains into a Qualified Opportunity Zone to delay paying taxes. These zones offer special tax benefits, and if you hold the investment long enough, you might not have to pay taxes on part of the gains.

Be sure to check the deadlines and rules for these investments to get the most benefits. Researching the specific zones and projects available can also help you align your financial goals with your tax-saving strategies.

8. Think About International Tax Strategies

If you're heavily involved in cryptocurrency, moving to a country with better tax policies might help. Some countries, like Portugal and Malta, have friendlier tax rules for crypto. However, if you're a U.S. citizen, you'll need to consider expatriation rules and possible exit taxes before making a move.

This strategy isn't for everyone, but for high-level investors, it can lead to significant tax savings. Make sure to weigh the pros and cons of relocating and consult a tax advisor who understands international tax law.

9. Work with a Tax Expert

Crypto taxes can be tricky, and the rules change often. A tax professional who knows about cryptocurrency can help you find the best strategies and stay out of trouble with the IRS. They can also keep you updated on new laws that might affect your plans.

Having an expert on your side can save you time and money. They can also help you prepare for audits or respond to IRS inquiries if they arise. With professional advice, you're less likely to make costly mistakes or miss out on opportunities to save.

By following these tax-saving tips, you can keep more of your crypto earnings while staying within the law. As cryptocurrency rules and regulations change, staying informed and planning ahead will help you make the most of your investments. Checking your financial plans regularly and getting advice from experts can make a big difference in how much you save. Regular reviews of your crypto portfolio and strategies will ensure you're always ahead of the game.

Chapter 18: What Records Do I Need to Keep for Tax Audits?

Section 1: IRS Audit Triggers

Understanding what might make the IRS take a closer look at your taxes is a crucial part of staying prepared. The IRS doesn't reveal every reason it selects tax returns for audits, but there are certain patterns and actions that often raise red flags. Being aware of these triggers can help you avoid making errors that might attract attention and lead to additional scrutiny.

1. Income Doesn't Match Records

The IRS receives copies of forms like W-2s and 1099s directly from employers, clients, and other payers. If the income you report on your tax return doesn't match these records, it's likely to prompt an audit. Always ensure you report all sources of income, including side gigs, freelance work, or any irregular earnings. Double-check your records and use a reliable method, like accounting software, to reconcile all income before filing your return. Keeping detailed records of payment confirmations, invoices, and contracts can also provide essential support if questioned.

2. Big Deductions or Frequent Losses

Claiming deductions that seem unusually high compared to your income can signal a problem to the IRS. Similarly, consistently reporting business losses over several years might make them question whether your business is actually a for-profit venture. While you're entitled to claim every legitimate deduction, you need solid evidence to back up these claims. Save receipts, invoices, and any contracts related to the expenses you're deducting. Keeping an organized and categorized expense tracking system can make it easier to justify your deductions and show their accuracy if audited.

3. Unusual or High Charitable Donations

Charitable giving is admirable, but if your donations are unusually high compared to your income or lack proper documentation, the IRS might investigate. Make sure to keep all receipts, donation letters from the organizations, and relevant bank statements. Additionally, confirm that the charities you support are registered and approved by the IRS to ensure your deductions are valid. For larger donations, consider getting an appraisal or additional documentation to support your claims.

4. Home Office Deduction Errors

The home office deduction is one of the most beneficial for small business owners, but it's also one of the most frequently misused. To qualify, the space must be used exclusively and regularly for business purposes. If the size of your home office deduction seems too large or lacks proper records, it may raise suspicion. Keep detailed documentation, including photos of your office setup, floor plans showing its dimensions, and a log of business activities conducted in the space. These details can be invaluable if you need to prove your claim.

5. Cash-Intensive Businesses

Businesses that handle a lot of cash, such as restaurants, salons, or repair shops, often face additional scrutiny because cash transactions are harder to trace. To avoid issues, maintain daily sales logs, use reliable point-of-sale systems, and reconcile your accounts regularly. Having a well-documented paper trail of all cash inflows and outflows can show that your records are accurate and complete. Regularly reviewing your own records can also help you identify and correct any mistakes early.

6. Large Cash Transactions

If your business deals with large cash payments, it's crucial to file Form 8300 for transactions over $10,000, as required by the IRS. Failing to report these transactions or having an unusual volume of them can lead to an audit. To stay compliant, document every large cash payment thoroughly, including details about the payer and the purpose of the payment. Retaining receipts, contracts, and even notes about the transactions can demonstrate that you're following the rules.

7. Higher Income Levels

The more money you or your business earns, the higher the likelihood of an audit. The IRS often focuses on higher earners because the stakes for unpaid taxes are greater. If your income exceeds $200,000 annually, it's wise to take extra care with your tax filings. Consider working with a tax professional to ensure accuracy and compliance, and to identify any potential issues before they arise.

8. Foreign Accounts or Business Activities

If you have foreign bank accounts or are involved in international business, you may face closer scrutiny, especially if you fail to file required forms like the FBAR (Foreign Bank Account Report) or Form 8938 for foreign assets. Always report foreign income, and keep detailed records of your accounts and transactions. Documentation such as bank statements, contracts, and correspondence with foreign institutions can be vital if the IRS reviews your activities.

9. Misclassified Workers

Misclassifying employees as independent contractors to avoid paying payroll taxes is a common mistake that can trigger an audit. The IRS has specific rules for determining whether someone is an employee or a contractor. Make sure you understand these rules and classify your workers correctly. Keep written agreements and records of payments to contractors or employees to demonstrate your compliance.

10. Rounded Numbers on Returns

Using rounded numbers, like $5,000 or $10,000, on your tax return may make it look like you're estimating instead of reporting actual amounts. This can raise suspicion and prompt further investigation. To avoid this, always use exact numbers when reporting income and expenses. Utilize accounting tools or software that calculate accurate figures directly from your records to minimize errors.

11. Mixing Personal and Business Expenses

Blurring the lines between personal and business expenses is a common issue for small business owners. To avoid this, keep personal and business accounts completely separate. Use a dedicated business bank account and credit card to ensure that only legitimate business expenses are being claimed. Keeping itemized receipts and maintaining detailed expense reports can help substantiate your claims during an audit.

12. Late or Amended Tax Returns

Consistently filing late or frequently amending your tax returns can draw unwanted attention from the IRS. To stay on track, set reminders for tax deadlines and aim to file your return accurately the first time. Regularly reviewing your financial records throughout the year can reduce the likelihood of errors and late filings. If you do need to amend a return, include a clear explanation and supporting documents to minimize any potential issues.

By understanding these common audit triggers, you can reduce your chances of being audited and focus on running your business without unnecessary stress. Taking proactive steps, like keeping thorough records, seeking professional tax advice, and staying up-to-date with IRS guidelines, can provide peace of mind. Even if you're selected for an audit, having well-organized and complete documentation can make the process smoother and easier to navigate. The next section will explain in detail which records you should keep to be fully prepared for an audit.

Section 2: Essential Records for Audit Readiness

Getting ready for a possible IRS audit means keeping your business records organized and easy to access. Good recordkeeping not only helps you follow the rules but also makes your day-to-day work smoother and reduces stress during an audit. Here's a breakdown of the key records you should keep and why they matter:

1. Income Records

- **Invoices:** Save all invoices you send to customers, clients, or tenants. Whether these are paper or digital, make sure they're numbered in order and show the date, who the customer is, and what goods or services you provided.

- **Receipts:** Keep receipts for any money you receive, whether it's cash, checks, or electronic payments. This helps make sure your income matches what you report.

- **Bank Statements:** Hold on to statements for your business bank accounts, including deposits, withdrawals, and transfers. These should match your other financial records.

- **Sales Records:** Track all sales with detailed reports from your point-of-sale system or sales logs. If you have more than one way of earning money, keep records for each source.

2. Expense Records

- **Receipts for Purchases:** Save receipts for all things you buy for your business, like office supplies or software. Also, keep any related documents like purchase orders or payment confirmations.

- **Vendor Invoices:** Keep bills from suppliers and contractors, especially for big or regular expenses. These support your deductions and show who you're working with.

- **Credit Card Statements:** Hang on to business credit card statements and label expenses clearly so you know what each one was for.

3. Payroll Records

- **Employee W-2s and Contractor 1099s:** Keep copies of forms you give to employees and independent contractors. These show you're following tax rules.

- **Pay Stubs:** Save detailed records of what you pay employees, including regular pay, overtime, and bonuses.

- **Tax Withholding Records:** Keep proof of taxes withheld and paid for employees, like Social Security and Medicare.

4. Tax Filings

- **Income Tax Returns:** Hold onto all filed tax returns for federal, state, and local taxes. They're a snapshot of your business's income and deductions.

- **Sales Tax Filings:** Save records of sales tax payments and reports, especially if you do business in different states.

- **Payroll Tax Filings:** Keep copies of payroll tax forms like Form 941 and Form 940. These should match your payroll records.

5. Asset Records

- **Purchase Receipts:** Keep proof of what you paid for business assets like vehicles, equipment, or furniture. Add warranty info or maintenance records if needed.

- **Depreciation Schedules:** Save records showing how your assets lose value over time. These should match your tax filings.

- **Sale Records:** If you sell any assets, document the sale, including the price and any profit or loss.

6. Loan and Debt Records

- **Loan Agreements:** Save signed copies of loans, including details like interest rates and repayment terms.

- **Payment Records:** Keep proof of payments made on loans and how much interest was paid. Include records for refinancing if that applies.

7. Contracts and Agreements

- **Leases:** Keep lease agreements for property or equipment, including updates or changes.
- **Service Contracts:** Save agreements with contractors, vendors, or consultants to support expense claims and clarify responsibilities.
- **Partnership or Operating Agreements:** Keep current copies of these documents to prove how your business is set up and how profits are shared.

8. Mileage Logs

- If you deduct vehicle expenses, keep a log of all business trips. Include the date, purpose, and miles driven. You can use apps or spreadsheets to make this easier. Don't forget to save related receipts, like tolls.

9. Home Office Documentation (if it applies)

- **Utility Bills:** Save bills for electricity, water, and internet. Highlight the portion that's for your home office.
- **Square Footage:** Write down how much space you use for your office compared to your whole home. Photos of your workspace can help too.

10. Proof of Compliance

- **Licenses and Permits:** Keep copies of any licenses or permits your business needs. Make sure they're up to date.

- **Insurance Policies:** Save current and old insurance policies for things like liability or workers' compensation. Include proof of payment and any claims you've made.

Tips for Keeping Records:

- **Go Digital:** Scan paper documents and save them digitally to avoid losing them. Use secure cloud storage or encrypted drives to protect sensitive data.

- **Know How Long to Keep Records:** Follow IRS rules. Usually, keep records for three years, but sometimes up to seven. Keep anything about assets as long as you own them.

- **Do Regular Checkups:** Look over your records often to make sure they're accurate and complete. Fix any gaps right away.

- **Stay Organized:** Use folders, both physical and digital, to label and sort documents by type and year. For digital files, keep track of updates with version control.

By keeping these records in order, you'll be ready to handle any audit smoothly. This preparation shows professionalism and helps keep your business running with fewer worries.

Section 3: How to Organize and Store Documents Securely

Keeping your business documents organized and safe is important to be ready for a tax audit. By using helpful tools, sorting your records, and protecting them properly, you can make this process simple and effective. Here's a step-by-step guide to help you manage your documents easily:

1. Use Digital Tools for Document Management

Switching to digital storage can make it easier to keep track of your records and prevent them from getting lost or damaged. Here's how to use digital tools:

- **Scanning and Saving:** Get a good scanner or use apps like Adobe Scan or CamScanner on your phone to turn paper documents into digital files. This way, you always have a copy you can access.

- **Simple File Names:** Name your files in a way that's easy to understand, like "2024-01-15_Rent_Invoice." This helps you quickly find what you need.

- **Cloud Storage:** Use secure online storage like Google Drive or Dropbox. These let you save, share, and access your records from anywhere.

- **Accounting Software:** Tools like QuickBooks and Xero can help you attach receipts and other documents to your transactions, keeping everything in one place.

- **Automated Sorting:** Apps like Dext or Hubdoc can scan and organize your receipts for you, saving time and effort.

2. Categorize Records by Type

Sorting your records into groups makes it easier to find them during an audit. You can use categories like these:

- **Income Records:** Save sales receipts, invoices, and bank deposit slips. Make sure all income matches what's in your financial records.

- **Expense Records:** Organize receipts, vendor invoices, and credit card statements. Sort them into categories like travel, supplies, or utilities.

- **Payroll Records:** Keep employee W-2 forms, contractor 1099s, and records of taxes you've paid for payroll.

- **Tax Filings:** Store copies of past tax returns, payment proof, and any letters from the IRS.

- **Legal and Financial Documents:** Include contracts, business licenses, and loan agreements in this category.

3. Know How Long to Keep Records

You don't need to keep every record forever. Here's a simple guide for how long to hold onto things:

- **Three Years:** Most tax-related documents can be thrown out after three years.

- **Six Years:** Keep records for six years if there's a big error in your reported income.

- **Seven Years:** Documents about bad debts or worthless investments should be kept for seven years.

- **Forever:** Keep records like payroll taxes and anything related to fraud indefinitely.

4. Keep Your Documents Safe

Protecting your records from theft or loss is very important. Here's how to secure them:

- **Physical Documents:** Use locked cabinets for paper records. Only allow trusted people to access them.

- **Digital Documents:**
    - Use strong passwords with a mix of letters, numbers, and symbols.
    - Turn on two-factor authentication for added security.
    - Keep your software updated to fix security issues.
    - Encrypt sensitive files to prevent unauthorized access.
    - Install antivirus software on all devices that store or access records.

5. Review Your Records Regularly

Checking your records often ensures they're up-to-date and complete. Here are some habits to adopt:

- **Quarterly Reviews:** Match your records with financial statements every few months to make sure everything lines up.
- **Yearly Cleanup:** At the end of each year, archive old records to free up space but make sure you're still following retention rules.
- **Practice Audits:** Do a mock audit to spot any gaps in your records and fix them early.
- **Teach Your Team:** Train your employees on good record-keeping practices and make sure they're consistent.

6. Back Up Your Records

Having backups of your documents can save you in case of emergencies. Here's how to stay prepared:

- **Cloud Backups:** Use online backup services to automatically save your files. Check regularly to make sure backups are working.
- **External Drives:** Keep copies of important files on an external hard drive or USB stick, stored in a safe place.
- **Offsite Storage:** For extra security, store physical backups in a separate location, like a bank's safe deposit box.

- **Double Protection:** Have at least two backups in different places to reduce the chance of losing everything. Test your backups now and then to make sure they work.

By following these steps, you'll not only be ready for a tax audit but also have a well-organized system that makes managing your business easier. Staying on top of your records will save you time, lower stress, and give you peace of mind.

Chapter 19: What Tax-Saving Strategies Can I Use to Reduce My Liability Legally?

Section 1: Overview of Common Tax-Saving Strategies

Running a small business involves managing numerous financial obligations, and taxes are among the most significant. However, with careful planning and a clear understanding of available strategies, you can significantly reduce your tax liability while staying fully compliant with the law. Here's an overview of some of the most common and effective tax-saving strategies. By employing these approaches, small business owners can save money, reinvest in their businesses, and gain a greater sense of financial security.

1. Choose the Right Business Structure

The legal structure of your business — whether it's a sole proprietorship, partnership, LLC, S-Corp, or C-Corp — has a significant impact on how much tax you'll owe. The choice you make can influence your tax obligations, liability exposure, and even eligibility for certain deductions and credits. For example:

- **S-Corps** can allow business owners to take a combination of salary and distributions, which may reduce payroll tax liability and create an opportunity to optimize overall taxation.
- **LLCs** offer flexibility in taxation and can be treated as sole proprietorships, partnerships, or

corporations, depending on what's most advantageous. This adaptability can provide strategic tax planning benefits as your business grows.

- **C-Corps** may benefit from a flat corporate tax rate, but they are also subject to double taxation on profits and dividends, which can be mitigated through careful planning.

Evaluate your current structure regularly to ensure it aligns with your financial goals and tax strategy. Consulting with a tax professional can provide valuable insights into whether it's time to make a change.

2. Take Advantage of Retirement Contributions

Contributing to retirement accounts not only helps secure your future but also offers immediate tax benefits. Retirement plans provide multiple options for small business owners and self-employed individuals:

- **401(k) Plans**: Contributions are tax-deductible and grow tax-deferred until retirement. Employers may also provide matching contributions to further enhance the tax benefits for employees.

- **SEP IRAs** and **SIMPLE IRAs**: Ideal for small businesses, these accounts allow higher contribution limits compared to traditional IRAs, offering an excellent opportunity to reduce taxable income significantly.

- **Solo 401(k)**: A great option for self-employed individuals, offering generous contribution limits and the flexibility to include both employee and employer contributions, maximizing the tax advantage.

Consider automating contributions or increasing them annually to ensure you're taking full advantage of these tax-saving tools.

3. Claim All Available Business Deductions

Small business owners can deduct a wide range of expenses directly related to their business. These deductions can significantly reduce taxable income and enhance cash flow. Common deductible expenses include:

- Office supplies and equipment
- Professional fees (e.g., legal and accounting services)
- Marketing and advertising expenses, including digital campaigns
- Travel costs for business purposes, such as lodging and transportation
- Depreciation on business equipment and vehicles, which can be accelerated under specific rules

Accurate record-keeping is essential to ensure you can substantiate these deductions if audited. Utilizing software or professional bookkeeping services can simplify this process and ensure no eligible expense is overlooked.

4. Leverage Tax Credits

Tax credits reduce your tax bill dollar-for-dollar and are often more valuable than deductions. Unlike deductions, which lower taxable income, credits directly reduce the amount of tax owed. Some common credits for small businesses include:

- **Research and Development (R&D) Credit**: Encourages innovation by rewarding businesses for developing new products or processes. Even small businesses can qualify if they invest in improving their offerings.

- **Work Opportunity Tax Credit (WOTC)**: Offers incentives for hiring individuals from certain target groups, such as veterans or individuals receiving government assistance.

- **Energy Efficiency Credits**: Available for businesses that invest in renewable energy systems, such as solar panels, or upgrade to energy-efficient equipment. These credits often align with long-term cost savings.

Research industry-specific credits that might apply to your business, as there are often lesser-known opportunities available.

5. Utilize Depreciation and Section 179 Expensing

Instead of spreading the cost of expensive assets over several years, you may be able to deduct the entire cost in the year of purchase using Section 179 expensing. This can be particularly advantageous for businesses investing in significant capital assets like machinery, technology, or vehicles.

- **Bonus Depreciation** rules allow additional accelerated deductions for certain types of property, providing immediate tax benefits. This rule applies even if the asset is financed.

- Ensure accurate records are kept for all qualifying purchases, as detailed documentation is required to support these claims during audits.

6. Employ Family Members

If you hire family members to work in your business, you can deduct their salaries as a business expense, provided the compensation is reasonable and the work is legitimate. This strategy can have added tax advantages:

- For sole proprietors and LLCs taxed as sole proprietorships, wages paid to your children under 18 are often exempt from Social Security and Medicare taxes.

- Hiring a spouse may provide eligibility for additional benefits, such as retirement contributions or health insurance coverage.

This approach can keep income within the family while reducing your overall tax liability.

7. Plan for Health Insurance Costs

Offering health insurance to yourself and your employees can provide significant tax advantages. Options include:

- **Health Reimbursement Arrangements (HRAs)**: Allows employers to reimburse employees tax-free for medical expenses. This can also benefit owners in certain cases.

- **Self-Employed Health Insurance Deduction**: Sole proprietors can deduct premiums paid for themselves and their families, reducing their adjusted gross income.

- **Health Savings Accounts (HSAs)**: Pairing a high-deductible health plan with an HSA can offer pre-tax contributions, tax-free growth, and tax-free withdrawals for qualified expenses.

8. Maximize Home Office Deductions

If you work from home, you may qualify for a home office deduction. Ensure the space is used exclusively and regularly for business to claim expenses like:

- A portion of your rent or mortgage interest
- Utilities, including internet and electricity
- Maintenance and repairs related to the office space

The IRS offers a simplified deduction option based on square footage, which can be easier to calculate and document.

9. Manage Inventory and Cost of Goods Sold (COGS)

Effective inventory management can impact your taxable income. Strategies like choosing the appropriate inventory valuation method (e.g., FIFO, LIFO) can align with your business's cash flow needs and tax planning. Additionally, identifying obsolete or unsellable inventory can result in write-offs, further reducing taxable income.

By understanding and implementing these strategies, small business owners can retain more of their hard-earned money and invest it back into their businesses. Regular consultation with tax professionals, combined with proactive planning and record-keeping, ensures that you're not only compliant with tax laws but also making the most of every opportunity to minimize your tax burden.

Section 2: Commonly Overlooked Tax Saving Strategies

Many people miss chances to save on taxes simply because they don't know about certain strategies. By learning about these methods, you can take steps to lower your tax bill while staying within the rules. Below is a detailed guide to help you maximize your savings and avoid unnecessary tax burdens:

1. Use the Qualified Business Income Deduction (QBID)

If you own a small business, work as a freelancer, or are self-employed, you might qualify for the Qualified Business Income Deduction (QBID). This deduction allows you to write off up to 20% of your qualified business income. However, there are rules and income limits, especially for service-based businesses like law firms or consulting practices. To fully understand your eligibility and maximize this deduction, it's smart to work with a tax expert who can guide you through the specifics.

Additionally, reviewing your business structure regularly can provide extra savings. For example, restructuring your business as an S-corporation could help you qualify for QBID while saving on payroll taxes. This strategy requires careful planning, so seek professional advice.

2. Open a Health Savings Account (HSA) or Flexible Spending Account (FSA)

Health Savings Accounts (HSAs) and Flexible Spending Accounts (FSAs) are excellent tools to save on taxes while preparing for medical expenses. HSAs offer a triple tax benefit: contributions are tax-deductible, the money grows tax-free, and you don't pay taxes on withdrawals for qualified medical expenses. If you have a high-deductible health insurance plan, consider contributing the maximum allowed by law for long-term and short-term tax advantages.

FSAs allow you to set aside pre-tax dollars for medical or dependent care expenses. While FSAs provide immediate savings, remember they have a "use-it-or-lose-it" rule, meaning any unused funds may be forfeited. Plan carefully to ensure your contributions align with anticipated expenses.

3. Hire Your Family Members

If you own a business, employing family members can be an effective tax-saving strategy. For example, wages paid to children under 18 in a family-owned business are not subject to Social Security and Medicare taxes if your business is a sole proprietorship or a partnership owned by the parents. This not only reduces your taxable income but also allows your children to start saving or investing their earnings.

To ensure compliance, assign real work responsibilities to family members and pay them a reasonable wage based on the tasks performed. Keep detailed records, including timesheets and job descriptions, to protect yourself in case of an audit.

4. Deduct Business Start-Up Costs

Starting a business involves significant expenses, many of which are tax-deductible. The IRS allows you to deduct up to $5,000 in start-up costs and another $5,000 in organizational expenses in the first year of operation. Qualifying expenses include market research, advertising, and legal fees. If your start-up costs exceed these limits, you can amortize the remaining expenses over a 15-year period.

Planning your expenses strategically during the initial stages of your business can maximize your deductions. Keep thorough records of all costs incurred during the set-up phase to claim these benefits.

5. Plan Charitable Donations

Donating to charity can provide both personal satisfaction and significant tax savings. Instead of donating cash, consider gifting appreciated assets like stocks or mutual funds. By doing so, you can avoid capital gains taxes on the appreciation and claim the full market value as a deduction.

For those who wish to make large charitable contributions, setting up a donor-advised fund can be beneficial. This allows you to take an immediate tax deduction for your donation while distributing the funds to charities over time. Bunching donations into a single year can also help you exceed the standard deduction threshold, increasing your tax savings.

6. Use Education Tax Credits

If you or a dependent is pursuing higher education, you might qualify for education-related tax credits. The American Opportunity Tax Credit (AOTC) provides up to $2,500 per student for undergraduate expenses, while the Lifetime Learning Credit offers up to $2,000 annually for tuition and fees related to job training or continuing education.

Even if you're not enrolled in a formal program, work-related courses or certifications may qualify as deductible business expenses. Save receipts for tuition, books, and other costs to claim these valuable credits.

7. Get Home Energy Tax Credits

Improving your home's energy efficiency can save you money on utility bills and taxes. Federal tax credits are available for installing solar panels, geothermal heating systems, or energy-efficient windows and doors. These credits can significantly reduce the cost of home upgrades.

Additionally, many states offer rebates or incentives for energy-efficient improvements. Research both federal and state programs to take full advantage of these opportunities.

8. Maximize State and Local Tax Deductions

While the federal State and Local Tax (SALT) deduction is capped at $10,000, you can optimize this benefit by carefully tracking property taxes, state income taxes, and sales taxes. Consider prepaying property taxes or other eligible expenses before the end of the year to maximize your deduction within the allowed limit.

If you operate in multiple states, consult a tax professional to ensure you're not overpaying state taxes. Strategic planning can help minimize your overall tax burden.

9. Time Your Income and Expenses

Timing your income and expenses strategically can make a big difference in your tax liability. For example, if you're close to moving into a higher tax bracket, consider delaying invoicing clients until the next tax year. Similarly, prepaying expenses like rent, insurance, or utilities can reduce your taxable income for the current year.

This strategy is particularly useful for businesses on a cash basis accounting method. Planning ahead and reviewing your cash flow can ensure you're making the most of timing-based deductions.

10. Pick the Right Filing Status

Your filing status plays a major role in determining your tax bill. While married couples typically benefit from filing jointly, there are situations where filing separately might be advantageous—such as when one spouse has high medical expenses or other deductions limited by income. Evaluate both options to see which status saves you the most.

For single taxpayers, consider if you qualify for head of household status, which offers a higher standard deduction and lower tax rates if you support a dependent.

11. Offset Gains with Losses

Investment losses can help you reduce your tax bill by offsetting gains. If your losses exceed your gains, you can deduct up to $3,000 of the remaining amount against your ordinary income. Unused losses can be carried forward to future tax years, providing ongoing tax benefits.

Be mindful of the wash-sale rule, which prevents you from claiming a loss if you repurchase the same or a substantially identical asset within 30 days. Proper planning can help you maximize the benefits of loss harvesting.

12. Save for Retirement

Contributing to retirement accounts like a 401(k), IRA, or SEP IRA is one of the most effective ways to reduce your taxable income while preparing for the future. Self-employed individuals can take advantage of higher contribution limits with accounts like Solo 401(k)s or SIMPLE IRAs. If you're over 50, make use of catch-up contributions to save even more.

Consider consulting a financial advisor to determine the best retirement savings strategy for your situation. Maximizing your contributions can lead to substantial tax savings while securing your long-term financial stability.

By applying these often-overlooked strategies, you can significantly reduce your tax liability and keep more of your hard-earned money. Regularly consulting with a tax professional ensures you're staying compliant with current laws and taking advantage of all available opportunities.

Section 3: Long-Term Planning to Minimize Taxes

Effective tax planning is not just about addressing your current tax obligations; it's about making strategic decisions that minimize taxes over the long haul. By adopting forward-thinking strategies, you can align your financial goals with tax efficiency, ensuring you keep more of what you earn while building wealth. Below are some comprehensive approaches to ensure your tax liability stays as low as possible in the years to come:

1. Utilize Depreciation Strategies

Investing in assets like equipment or property can provide substantial tax benefits through depreciation. By planning the timing and scope of these investments, you can take advantage of deductions that align with your highest-income years, providing the greatest impact.

- **Bonus Depreciation:** This method allows businesses to immediately expense a significant portion of the cost of eligible assets, such as machinery or vehicles, in the year they are placed in service. Bonus depreciation can significantly reduce taxable income in the short term while incentivizing reinvestment.

- **Section 179 Deduction:** This option permits businesses to deduct the full purchase price of qualifying equipment and software, up to a specific limit, rather than depreciating it over several years. Long-term tax planning involves strategically timing these deductions to maximize benefits when your earnings peak.

- **Regular Depreciation:** For assets not qualifying for accelerated options, traditional depreciation schedules spread deductions across several years. Consistent planning ensures you're maximizing value while staying compliant with IRS regulations.

2. Leverage Tax-Efficient Investments

Tax-efficient investing plays a crucial role in minimizing the taxes you owe while growing your wealth. By carefully selecting and managing your portfolio, you can reduce both immediate and long-term tax liabilities.

- **Tax-Advantaged Accounts:** Contributing to accounts like Roth IRAs, Traditional IRAs, or Health Savings Accounts (HSAs) not only reduces current taxable income (in the case of HSAs and Traditional IRAs) but also grows your investments tax-deferred or tax-free, depending on the account type.

- **Municipal Bonds:** These bonds, issued by state and local governments, generate interest income that is typically exempt from federal taxes and, in some cases, state and local taxes. They're an excellent choice for individuals in higher tax brackets.

- **Tax-Loss Harvesting:** By selling investments at a loss, you can offset capital gains and even a portion of your regular income. Implementing this strategy annually can make a significant difference over time, especially in volatile markets.

- **Dividend Stocks and ETFs:** Focusing on qualified dividends can lower your tax rate compared to ordinary income, as they are often taxed at favorable rates.

3. Plan for Succession and Estate Taxes

If you intend to transfer your business or other assets to heirs, proactive estate planning can prevent substantial tax obligations for your beneficiaries while preserving your legacy.

- **Gifting Strategies:** The IRS allows annual tax-free gifts up to a certain threshold per recipient. Utilizing this strategy over time can significantly reduce the size of your taxable estate.

- **Trusts:** Establishing trusts, such as irrevocable life insurance trusts (ILITs) or charitable remainder trusts, can protect your assets from estate taxes while ensuring they're distributed according to your wishes.

- **Lifetime Exemptions:** Take advantage of the federal lifetime exemption, which permits individuals to transfer a large amount of wealth tax-free over their lifetime. Pair this with strategic gifting to maximize tax savings.

- **Business Succession Plans:** For business owners, succession planning should include strategies to reduce taxes during the transfer, such as family limited partnerships or installment sales.

4. Stay Informed About Tax Law Changes

Tax laws are constantly evolving, and staying informed can ensure your strategies remain effective and compliant. Being proactive about adjustments in the tax code can open opportunities to optimize your plans.

- **Monitor Legislative Changes:** Changes to tax rates, deductions, or credits can directly affect your planning. Staying updated helps you take timely action.

- **Temporary Tax Breaks:** Some tax incentives are only available for a limited time. Examples include bonus depreciation or pandemic-related tax relief programs. Make the most of these opportunities while they last.

- **Consult Experts:** Regularly review your strategy with a CPA or tax professional who can help interpret how new laws impact your financial situation and adjust your plans accordingly.

5. Work with a Tax Professional

Long-term tax planning is complex, requiring knowledge of ever-changing regulations and their implications for your specific circumstances. Engaging a tax professional ensures your strategies are both effective and compliant.

- **Tailored Advice:** A tax advisor or CPA can analyze your unique financial situation to create a personalized plan that optimizes your tax savings while aligning with your goals.

- **Proactive Adjustments:** Professionals can identify potential challenges or opportunities in advance, helping you mitigate risks or capitalize on benefits.

- **Audit Preparedness:** By working with a professional, you'll have peace of mind knowing your financial records are accurate and defensible in the event of an audit.

By embracing these long-term strategies, you'll not only reduce your tax liability year over year but also create a more stable and prosperous financial future. A proactive approach to tax planning is one of the most effective ways to build and preserve wealth, ensuring your business and personal finances thrive over the long term.

Conclusion

Taking care of your small business finances might feel overwhelming at first, but it's a key part of making sure your business succeeds. By learning the basics of bookkeeping, taxes, and financial planning, you're setting yourself up for growth, stability, and long-term success. Managing money isn't just about numbers—it's about creating a strong foundation to reach your goals and handle challenges with confidence.

In this book, we've talked about many topics, like picking the best bookkeeping tools, understanding tax rules, and planning for the future. Each section was made to give you simple advice, helpful tips, and the confidence to handle your business finances. By using what you've learned here, you can turn managing your money into a powerful tool for success.

Here are some key points to keep in mind:

1. **Stay Organized and On Top of Things**: Good habits and accurate records are the basics of any successful business. Check your accounts regularly and keep your records updated. Being organized saves time and helps you see how your business is doing, so you can make smart choices.

2. **Know Your Tax Responsibilities**: Whether it's paying quarterly taxes, using deductions, or choosing the right type of business structure, knowing your tax responsibilities can save you money and reduce stress. Staying on top of taxes

also helps you avoid penalties and take advantage of savings.

3. **Use Financial Reports**: Reports like profit and loss statements and balance sheets aren't just numbers—they help you measure how your business is doing, plan ahead, and make smart decisions. Reviewing these reports regularly can show you trends, highlight areas to improve, and give you reasons to celebrate your wins.

4. **Get Professional Help When Needed**: While many small business owners can handle their own finances, it's okay to ask for help when things get tricky. A bookkeeper, tax expert, or financial advisor can give you clear advice, help you stay on track, and show you opportunities you might not notice on your own. Working with experts can save time and help you focus on growing your business.

5. **Plan for Growth**: Managing your finances isn't just about keeping up with today's needs—it's also about planning for the future. Use the tools and knowledge from this book to find opportunities to grow and make sure your financial plans match your goals. A good plan can help you expand your business while staying steady.

6. **Think Long-Term**: Running a business takes time and effort. The choices you make today—like buying tools, hiring staff, or deciding where to spend money—will affect your business for

years. Keep checking your financial strategies to make sure they still match your goals and changes in the market.

As you move forward, remember that managing your business finances is not a one-time task. It's something you need to do all the time. The effort you put in now will lead to a strong, successful business in the future. Celebrate your wins, learn from challenges, and keep improving. Managing money is a skill that grows with time, and every step you take brings you closer to mastering it.

Thank you for letting this book be part of your journey as a small business owner. We hope it has given you the tools, knowledge, and confidence to reach your goals. Here's to your success, growth, and a bright future!

Appendix 1: Sample Chart of Accounts

A well-organized Chart of Accounts (COA) is crucial for maintaining accurate financial records and ensuring that your bookkeeping aligns with industry standards. Below is a sample COA, which can be customized to suit the specific needs of your business.

General Chart of Accounts

Assets

1. **Current Assets**
    - 1000 Cash on Hand
    - 1010 Checking Account
    - 1020 Savings Account
    - 1030 Accounts Receivable
    - 1040 Inventory
    - 1050 Prepaid Expenses

2. **Fixed Assets**
    - 1500 Furniture and Equipment
    - 1510 Vehicles
    - 1520 Accumulated Depreciation

3. **Other Assets**
    - 1700 Security Deposits
    - 1710 Intangible Assets (e.g., Patents, Trademarks)

Liabilities
1. **Current Liabilities**
    - 2000 Accounts Payable
    - 2010 Credit Card Payable
    - 2020 Accrued Expenses
    - 2030 Sales Tax Payable
2. **Long-Term Liabilities**
    - 2500 Loans Payable
    - 2510 Mortgage Payable

Equity
1. **Owner's Equity**
    - 3000 Owner's Capital
    - 3010 Owner's Draws
2. **Retained Earnings**
    - 3100 Retained Earnings

Income
1. **Revenue**
    - 4000 Product Sales
    - 4010 Service Revenue
    - 4020 Discounts and Refunds

Expenses

1. **Cost of Goods Sold (COGS)**
    - 5000 Materials and Supplies
    - 5010 Direct Labor

2. **Operating Expenses**
    - 6000 Advertising and Marketing
    - 6010 Bank Fees
    - 6020 Depreciation Expense
    - 6030 Insurance Expense
    - 6040 Office Supplies
    - 6050 Professional Services (e.g., Legal, Accounting)
    - 6060 Rent or Lease Expense
    - 6070 Salaries and Wages
    - 6080 Utilities
    - 6090 Vehicle Expenses

3. **Other Expenses**
    - 6500 Interest Expense
    - 6510 Taxes and Licenses
    - 6520 Miscellaneous Expenses

This sample COA is a starting point. Depending on your business's nature, you may need to add, remove, or rename accounts. For instance, if you're in retail, you might add accounts for sales categories like "In-Store Sales" and "Online Sales." If you're in a service industry, you might emphasize accounts related to client services and subcontractors.

Sample COA for "Fresh Start LLC"

Type: Retail Store Business Structure: Limited Liability Company (LLC)

Assets

1. **Current Assets**
   - 1000 Cash on Hand
   - 1010 Checking Account
   - 1030 Accounts Receivable
   - 1040 Inventory (e.g., Clothing, Accessories)

2. **Fixed Assets**
   - 1500 Computer Equipment (e.g., Point-of-Sale System)
   - 1510 Office Furniture
   - 1520 Leasehold Improvements (e.g., Store Renovations)

Liabilities

1. **Current Liabilities**

- 2000 Accounts Payable (e.g., Vendor Invoices)
- 2010 Business Credit Card
- 2020 Deferred Revenue (e.g., Gift Cards)

2. **Long-Term Liabilities**
    - 2500 Start-Up Loan Payable

Equity

1. **Owner's Equity**
    - 3000 Owner's Investment

Income

1. **Revenue**
    - 4000 Sales Revenue (e.g., In-Store and Online Sales)

Expenses

1. **Cost of Goods Sold (COGS)**
    - 5000 Raw Materials (e.g., Fabric, Packaging)
    - 5010 Packaging Supplies

2. **Operating Expenses**
    - 6000 Advertising and Marketing (e.g., Social Media Ads)
    - 6010 Internet and Website Costs (e.g., E-commerce Hosting)

- 6020 Software Subscriptions (e.g., Accounting Software)
- 6030 Legal and Professional Fees
- 6040 Rent and Utilities (e.g., Storefront Lease)
- 6050 Wages and Salaries (e.g., Store Associates)

This COA is designed for "Fresh Start LLC," a retail start-up focused on selling clothing and accessories. As the business grows, additional accounts can be added to reflect more complex operations and transactions.

Appendix 2: Tax Deadlines and Calendars

Managing tax deadlines is a crucial aspect of running a small business. Missing deadlines can result in penalties and interest charges, which are both costly and stressful. Below is an outline of key tax deadlines and calendars to help you stay on track throughout the year.

Key Tax Deadlines for Small Businesses

January

- **January 15**: Deadline for the fourth estimated quarterly tax payment for the previous tax year (if applicable).
- **January 31**:
  - Deadline to distribute Form W-2 to employees and file them with the Social Security Administration.
  - Deadline to provide Form 1099-NEC to independent contractors and file them with the IRS.

March

- **March 15**:
  - Deadline for S Corporations and Partnerships to file their annual tax returns (Forms 1120-S and 1065, respectively) or file for a six-month extension.

- Deadline for S Corporations to provide Schedule K-1 to shareholders.

April

- **April 15** (or the next business day if it falls on a weekend or holiday):
    - Deadline for individuals, sole proprietors, and C Corporations to file income tax returns (Forms 1040 and 1120) or file for a six-month extension.
    - Deadline for first estimated quarterly tax payment for the current tax year.

June

- **June 15**: Deadline for second estimated quarterly tax payment for the current tax year.

September

- **September 15**:
    - Deadline for third estimated quarterly tax payment for the current tax year.
    - Deadline for S Corporations and Partnerships to file their extended tax returns (if an extension was requested).

October

- **October 15**:
  - Final deadline for individuals and C Corporations to file extended tax returns (if an extension was requested).

December

- **December 31**: Deadline for any year-end tax planning strategies, such as making retirement contributions or adjusting payroll to maximize deductions.

Tax Calendar Overview

Month	Deadline
January	Fourth quarterly tax payment, W-2 and 1099-NEC distribution
March	Tax returns for S Corps and Partnerships, Schedule K-1 distribution
April	Individual and C Corporation tax returns, first quarterly tax payment
June	Second quarterly tax payment
September	Third quarterly tax payment, extended S Corp and Partnership returns

October	Extended individual and C Corporation tax returns
December	Year-end planning strategies

Tips for Staying Organized

1. **Use a Tax Calendar**: Set reminders for all key dates in your business calendar to ensure no deadlines are missed.

2. **Consult a Professional**: If you are unsure about your tax obligations, consult a tax professional to guide you through the process.

3. **Automate Payments**: Whenever possible, set up automatic payments for estimated taxes to avoid last-minute stress.

4. **Track Expenses Year-Round**: Use bookkeeping software to stay on top of your income and expenses, making tax preparation easier.

By adhering to these deadlines and employing effective organizational tools, you can minimize stress and keep your business compliant with tax regulations.

Appendix 3: Resources for Small Business Owners

Starting and running a small business can be a rewarding but complex endeavor. Fortunately, a wide variety of tools, websites, and organizations are available to support small business owners in managing their operations effectively. Below is a curated list of resources to help with various aspects of small business ownership.

A. Tools for Small Business Owners

1. Bookkeeping and Accounting Tools

- **QuickBooks Online:** Comprehensive accounting software suitable for small businesses. Website: https://quickbooks.intuit.com.

- **Wave Accounting:** Free accounting and invoicing tool for small businesses. Website: https://www.waveapps.com.

- **Xero:** Cloud-based accounting software with robust reporting features. Website: https://www.xero.com.

2. Payroll Management Tools

- **Gusto:** Easy-to-use payroll and benefits management. Website: https://gusto.com.

- **ADP:** Scalable payroll services for businesses of all sizes. Website: https://www.adp.com.

- **OnPay:** Affordable payroll and HR solution for small businesses. Website: https://www.onpay.com.

3. Invoicing and Payment Tools

- **FreshBooks:** User-friendly invoicing and expense tracking software. Website: https://www.freshbooks.com.
- **PayPal for Business:** Online payments and invoicing for small businesses. Website: https://www.paypal.com/business.
- **Square:** Point-of-sale and payment processing tool. Website: https://www.squareup.com.

4. Project Management and Collaboration Tools

- **Trello:** Visual task management tool. Website: https://www.trello.com.
- **Asana:** Workflow management for teams. Website: https://www.asana.com.
- **Slack:** Communication tool for small business teams. Website: https://www.slack.com.

5. Marketing and Social Media Tools

- **Canva:** Graphic design platform for creating marketing materials. Website: https://www.canva.com.
- **Hootsuite:** Social media management and scheduling. Website: https://www.hootsuite.com.

- **Mailchimp:** Email marketing automation tool. Website: https://www.mailchimp.com.

B. Websites for Small Business Guidance

1. U.S. Small Business Administration (SBA)

Website: www.sba.gov

- Offers information on starting, funding, and managing a business.
- Provides access to loans, grants, and free business counseling.

2. SCORE

Website: www.score.org

- Free mentoring and workshops for small business owners.
- Wide range of templates and tools.

3. Internal Revenue Service (IRS)

Website: www.irs.gov

- Tax resources for small businesses and self-employed individuals.
- Information on tax deadlines, forms, and deductions.

4. Local Chamber of Commerce

Website: www.uschamber.com

- Networking opportunities and resources for local business communities.

5. National Association for the Self-Employed (NASE)

Website: www.nase.org

- Advocacy and benefits for self-employed individuals.
- Offers health insurance options and tax resources.

C. Professional Organizations

1. National Federation of Independent Business (NFIB)

Website: https://www.nfib.com

- Advocacy for small business rights and interests.
- Resources on compliance and best practices.

2. American Institute of Certified Public Accountants (AICPA)

Website: https://www.aicpa.org

- Guidance on financial and tax planning for small businesses.
- Resources for finding qualified CPAs.

3. Small Business Development Centers (SBDC)

Website: https://www.sba.gov/sbdc

- Free consulting and low-cost training for small business owners.
- Access to business plan templates and market research.

4. Women's Business Enterprise National Council (WBENC)

Website: https://www.wbenc.org

- Certification and resources for women-owned businesses.
- Networking opportunities and supplier diversity programs.

D. Industry-Specific Resources

Many industries have dedicated organizations or resources to support small business owners. Examples include:

- **National Restaurant Association:** Resources for restaurant and food service businesses. Website: https://www.restaurant.org.
- **American Bar Association (ABA):** Resources for solo and small law practices. Website: https://www.americanbar.org.

- **National Retail Federation (NRF):** Resources for retail business owners. Website: https://www.nrf.com.

By leveraging these tools, websites, and organizations, small business owners can build a strong foundation for success and navigate challenges with confidence.

www.ingramcontent.com/pod-product-compliance
Lightning Source LLC
Chambersburg PA
CBHW052141220526
45471CB00004B/1467